REGENTS RESTORATION DRAMA SERIES

General Editor: John Loftis

THE CARELESS HUSBAND

COLLEY CIBBER

The Careless Husband

Edited by

WILLIAM W. APPLETON

UNIVERSITY OF NEBRASKA PRESS · LINCOLN

Regents Restoration Drama Series

The Regents Restoration Drama Series, similar in objectives and format to the Regents Renaissance Drama Series, will provide soundly edited texts, in modern spelling, of the more significant English plays of the late seventeenth and early eighteenth centuries. The word "Restoration" is here used ambiguously and must be explained. If to the historian it refers to the period between 1660 and 1685 (or 1688), it has long been used by the student of drama in default of a more precise word to refer to plays belonging to the dramatic tradition established in the 1660's, weakening after 1700, and displaced in the 1730's. It is in this extended sense—imprecise though justified by academic custom—that the word is used in this series, which will include plays first produced between 1660 and 1737. Although these limiting dates are determined by political events, the return of Charles II (and the removal of prohibitions against the operation of theaters) and the passage of Walpole's Stage Licensing Act, they enclose a period of dramatic history having a coherence of its own in the establishment, development, and disintegration of a tradition.

Each text in the series is based on a fresh collation of the seventeenth- and eighteeth-century editions that might be presumed to have authority. The textual notes, which appear above the rule at the bottom of each page, record all substantive departures from the edition used as the copy-text. Variant substantive readings among contemporary editions are listed there as well. Editions later than the eighteenth century are referred to in the textual notes only when an emendation originating in some one of them is received into the text. Variants of accidentals (spelling, punctuation, capitalization) are not recorded in the notes. Contracted forms of characters' names are silently expanded in speech prefixes and stage directions, and, in the case of speech prefixes, are regularized. Additions to the stage directions of the copy-text are enclosed in brackets. Stage directions such as "within" or "aside" are enclosed in parentheses when they occur in the copy-text.

Spelling has been modernized along consciously conservative lines, but within the limits of a modernized text the linguistic quality of the original has been carefully preserved. Punctuation has been brought into accord with modern practices. The objective has been to achieve a balance between the generally light pointing of the old editions, and a system of punctuation which, without overloading the text with exclamation marks, semicolons, and dashes, will make the often loosely flowing verse and prose of the original syntactically intelligible to the modern reader. Dashes are regularly used only to indicate interrupted speeches, or shifts of address within a single speech.

Explanatory notes, chiefly concerned with glossing obsolete words and phrases, are printed below the textual notes at the bottom of each page. References to stage directions in the notes follow the admirable system of the Revels editions, whereby stage directions are keyed, decimally, to the line of the text before or after which they occur. Thus, a note on 0.2 has reference to the second line of the stage direction at the beginning of the scene in question. A note on 115.1 has reference to the first line of the stage direction following line 115 of the text of the relevant scene. Speech prefixes, and any stage directions attached to them, are keyed to the first line of accompanying dialogue.

JOHN LOFTIS

Stanford University

Contents

List of Abbreviations

Q1	First Quarto, 1705
Q2	Second Quarto, 1705
P	Plays (2 vols.), 1721
S.D.	stage direction
S.P.	speech prefix
om.	omitted

Introduction

The textual history of *The Careless Husband* is relatively uncompli-
cated. The first quarto of 1705 is a good text and the basis for subsequent editions. A second quarto, differing only in minor details,
appeared the same year. In the course of the next fifteen years three
more quarto editions appeared, but not until the publication of
Cibber's two-volume *Plays* in 1721 do we find any real textual
variations. These alterations, it has been assumed, were made by
Cibber himself, particularly since they occur most frequently in the
scenes in which Lord Foppington appears. The verbal changes are
frequent but they are, for the most part, minor—the transposition,
omission, or addition of a phrase or word. It is possible that Cibber
was guided by a desire to heighten and polish his dialogue; more
probably he was merely revising the earlier text to conform to the
actual stage text which had evolved in the course of performance.
The increased number of stage directions in the 1721 edition also
suggests that Cibber was trying to recreate for the reader, as far as
possible, the sense of actually being in the theater. The subsequent
duodecimo editions, based on the first quarto text, with some inter-
polations from the 1721 edition, are without interest. The first quarto
of 1705 has been used as the copy-text for this edition. The editor has
occasionally introduced, and duly noted, an important reading or
stage direction from the collected edition of 1721.

Looking back on nearly half a century in the theater as a playwright, actor, and manager, Colley Cibber wrote: "My Muse and
my spouse were equally prolific . . . the one was seldom the mother
of a child but, in the same year, the other made me the father of a
play." [1] As far as we can judge, Cibber began *The Careless Husband* in
1702, some months before the birth of his son, Theophilus. Cibber's
casual allusions to his Muse, "called up in the line of family duty,"
are characteristic of his tough, practical attitude toward the theater.

---

[1] *An Apology for the Life of Colley Cibber* (London, 1740), p. 153.

Ever on the lookout for suitable dramatic material, Cibber derived the key incident in *The Careless Husband*, Boswell tells us, from an actual episode that occurred in the household of his friends, Colonel and Mrs. Brett.

> Colonel Brett was reported to be too free in his gallantry with his Lady's maid. Mrs. Brett came into a room one day in her own house, and found the Colonel and her maid both fast asleep in two chairs. She tied a white handkerchief round her husband's neck, which was a sufficient proof that she had discovered his intrigue; but she never at any time took notice of it to him. This incident, as I am told, gave occasion to the well-wrought scene of Sir Charles and Lady Easy and Edging.[2]

Around this episode Cibber built his comedy, filling it out with the secondary plot—the wooing of an attractive coquette by a worthy but somewhat humorless young lord. But as Cibber's pen raced across the paper he found that the character of Lady Betty Modish, the coquette, increasingly dominated the play. It was a role that called for an actress of enormous charm who could humanize the part, as Mrs. Bracegirdle had done with Congreve's Millamant. Mrs. Verbruggen, who had shown her capacities in such roles as Lady Froth in *The Double Dealer* and Narcissa in *Love's Last Shift*, seemed ideally suited to the part. Cibber was at work on the play in the summer of 1703 when the Drury Lane company left London to perform at Bath. To his dismay, Mrs. Verbruggen pleaded indisposition and remained behind. Shortly afterwards, she died. Cibber put aside his manuscript, feeling that no other actress could do justice to the part, but in the course of the Bath engagement a comparative newcomer, Anne Oldfield, took the minor role of Leonora in Crowne's comedy *Sir Courtly Nice*. Her sparkling performance was a revelation, and Cibber realized that he had found Lady Betty. Soon after, he completed the play.[3]

It was produced at Drury Lane on December 7, 1704, and played sixteen times before the end of the season. The following season it had four performances, and during the next one five. Although not among the most frequently acted eighteenth-century comedies, in the course of the next century scarcely a year passed in which it was not performed two or three times, and anthologists regularly reprinted it in

[2] James Boswell, *The Life of Samuel Johnson* (London, 1791), I, 94 n.
[3] Cibber, *Apology*, pp. 175–176.

their collections. It was included in Lewis Hallam's repertory on his American tour, and virtually every well-known eighteenth-century actor and actress appeared in the play at one time or another—David Garrick, Charles Macklin, Henry Woodward, Peg Woffington, and Mrs. Abington—but it is associated primarily with Anne Oldfield.

In his *Apology* Cibber pays eloquent tribute to her.

> Whatever favorable reception this comedy has met with from the public, it would be unjust in me not to place a large share of it to the account of Mrs. Oldfield; not only from the uncommon excellence of her action, but even from her personal manner of conversing. There are many sentiments in the character of Lady Betty Modish that, I may almost say, were originally her own, or only dressed with a little more care than when they negligently fell from her lively humor.[4]

Sprightly in manner, with a melodious voice and expressive eyes which she had a trick of half-shutting for comic effect, she made the part so entirely her own that until her death in 1730 no other actress attempted it. Indeed, so closely was she associated with the role that it is difficult to disentangle her own life from that of the character she played. Besides the broad likenesses which Cibber noted, there were curious minor parallels as well. Mrs. Oldfield had passed a good part of the summer of 1703 in lodgings on the Castle grounds at Windsor, the scene of the play. Likewise, the tastes of Cibber's coquette accurately mirrored her own. Lady Betty's expression of distaste at the notion of being buried in woolen (IV.356) might be cited as an example of literature paralleling life: if Mrs. Oldfield is remembered at all today by the common reader it is probably because of Pope's caustic lines in his *Moral Essays* criticizing the folly of her burial in Brussels lace and flowered chintz.[5] But theatergoers took a more indulgent view of Mrs. Oldfield's addiction to worldly vanities, and for a generation she delighted them as Lady Betty.

At least two others in the original cast were, it would seem, equally effective. Cibber, as Lord Foppington, added yet another lively portrait to his gallery of coxcombs, and Robert Wilks, as Sir Charles Easy, brought to his role an airy good humor and elegance. The play was "acted to perfection," Steele tells us, "both by them

[4] *Ibid.*, p. 177.
[5] *Moral Essays: Epistle I*, ll. 246–251.

and all concerned in it." [6] For over twenty-five years Mrs. Oldfield, Cibber, and Wilks, supported usually by Mills as Lord Morelove and Mrs. Porter as Lady Easy, captivated audiences. Though the play contains only seven characters, they are all sharply etched and effectively contrasted. The least important role is that of Edging, Lady Easy's maid, but even this part is a good one, and Kitty Clive, Garrick's leading comedienne, later undertook it without any feeling that it was below her dignity. It is, in short, an ideal play for a repertory company, designed to show off both ensemble and individual acting.

But there were other reasons for the play's success. Cibber, in his usual fashion, had skilfully combined the old and the new. A number of the characters were familiar types in the theater. Lady Betty epitomizes the belles of Restoration comedy from Harriet in *The Man of Mode* to Millamant in *The Way of the World*. She takes an unabashed pleasure in the power of her beauty to reduce admirers to quivering helplessness and feels the traditional reluctance to abandon the assured pleasures of single life for the dubious joys of marriage. Lady Graveairs has her ancestry in that tempestuous group of cast-off mistresses, the Mrs. Loveits and Termagants of earlier comedy, the perpetual losers in the patterned world of society. Lord Foppington's derivation is similarly a familiar one; he stems from Molière's Mascarille and Etherege's Sir Fopling Flutter. In *Love's Last Shift* Cibber had reincarnated him as Sir Novelty Fashion, and in *The Relapse* Vanbrugh had raised him to the peerage. In *The Careless Husband* he is his usual ineffable comic self, yet Cibber also uses him for a more serious purpose. In the first scene in which he appears his relationship with his long-suffering wife is discussed at some length, and the playwright goes out of his way to criticize his behavior toward the unseen Lady Foppington.

All of these characters, conventional as they are, Cibber succeeds in endowing with genuine vitality. Sir Charles Easy, the careless husband, also seems, on the surface, to relate to earlier comedy, but he bears only a faint resemblance to the Restoration libertines. In *Love's Last Shift* Cibber had drawn the portrait of another erring husband, Loveless, reclaimed at the conclusion by a constant and resourceful wife. Sir Charles, like Loveless, is a man of the world with few illusions about human behavior, but from the beginning of the play he is drawn as a fundamentally good-hearted man, and his

6 *The Tatler*, No. 182: June 8, 1710.

final conversion is, consequently, more convincing than Loveless'. The scene between Sir Charles and Edging in Act V is Cibber's variant on the obligatory cuckolding scene of Restoration comedy, but it is fundamental to the moral design of the play.

Though Cibber was far from being in any serious sense a dramatist of ideas, his play is, nonetheless, often serious in tone. A notable feature of the play is the frequency with which the words "careless" and "easy" appear. They give a thematic unity to the main plot. Without in any sense formally exploring their philosophical implications, Cibber repeatedly uses them as points of reference. Like most of his worldly acquaintance he prized his ease and the opportunities it afforded him for self-gratification. At the same time he was far too shrewd not to recognize the advantages of certain social conventions. Beneath the comic surface of the play he repeatedly takes up the question—at what point does self-indulgent "ease" degenerate into irresponsible "carelessness"?

Lady Betty's yearning for power is another refraction of the same problem—the relation of the individual to society. If Lady Betty and Sir Charles move in the world of Hobbes, Lady Easy and Lord Morelove belong to the world of Shaftesbury. In essence, Cibber is trying to reconcile the cynicism of one with the humanitarianism of the other. Profligate in his own life, Cibber by temperament belonged to the Restoration, but he was well aware of the changes which were taking place. The story has often been told of the occasion when Mrs. Porter observed to him with some surprise that she could not understand how a man who could create characters of exemplary morality could at the same time show so little inclination to imitate them in his own life. The paradox did not bother Cibber. Inconsistencies between ideals and actualities were the stuff of life. To judge from his *Apology*, Cibber's married life was not an unhappy one, though he was scarcely an ideal husband. Sir Charles' weaknesses reflected his own, and it can hardly be a coincidence that Cibber's four major plays include scenes of marital reconciliation. That a man should want both a mistress and a wife seemed to him all too natural. One recalls, in this connection, Lord Hervey's famous account of Queen Caroline on her deathbed urging her husband, George II, to marry again. Between sobs he blurted out, "Non! J'aurai des maîtresses." The expiring queen wearily replied, "Ah, mon dieu! Cela n'empêche pas!"[7]

[7] John, Lord Hervey, *Some Materials towards Memoirs of the Reign of King George II*. Ed. Romney Sedgwick (London, 1931), III, 896.

Hervey describes the scene as scarcely credible, an opinion Cibber would not have shared.

In its focus on marriage his play is characteristic of the change in comedy inaugurated by Vanbrugh's *The Provoked Wife* (1697). Wearied of the pre-marital love-chase, dramatists turned instead to the post-marital quarrel, and their plays are dominated by a succession of provoked, jealous, and suspicious husbands and wives. They are scarcely new to the theater, but with the exception of an occasional couple like Rhodophil and Doralice in Dryden's *Marriage à la Mode*, the Restoration paid little attention to the relationship of man and woman after marriage. Cibber's comedies, by and large, begin where those of the Restoration leave off.

Though Cibber's own outlook was fundamentally skeptical, he was willing enough to let audience taste dictate the play's benevolent point of view and optimistic conclusion. Lady Easy's exemplary displays of wifely forbearance, rivaling those of the Patient Griselda, may not appeal to the modern reader, but they were evidently enjoyed by Cibber's contemporaries.[8] Most famous of these is the Steinkirk scene (V.v), in which Lady Easy discovers her husband and her maid, Edging, asleep in two chairs. Overcome by the evidence of her husband's infidelity, she bursts into a flood of appalling blank verse. After recovering her composure, she takes off her scarf and lays it gently over the head of her erring spouse. It is impossible to deny the artificiality of this episode, but the subsequent scenes are adroitly managed. Lady Easy's low-keyed dialogue with Edging, as they refashion a dress, has an undercurrent of real tension, and Sir Charles' final capitulation is shrewdly manipulated.

Largely because of the Steinkirk scene, Cibber's play has sometimes been called the first sentimental comedy, though it scarcely deserves that dubious honor. Eighteenth-century writers preferred to describe it as the first of the "genteel" comedies. As Thomas Davies, the actor and bookseller, put it, Cibber was "the first who introduced men and women of high quality on the stage, and gave them language and manners suitable to their rank and birth."[9] David Erskine Baker praised *The Careless Husband* for "perhaps the most elegant dialogue and the most perfect knowledge of the manners of persons in real high life extant in any dramatic piece that has yet appeared in any language whatever."[10] Even the waspish Horace Walpole credited

[8] Thomas Davies, *Dramatic Miscellanies* (London, 1784), III, 411, 432.
[9] *Ibid.*, III, 414. See also Boswell, *Johnson*, I, 473–474.
[10] *Biographia Dramatica* (London, 1782), II, 44.

Cibber with capturing the authentic tone of society.[11] Not everyone
has agreed. Congreve, both as a writer and as a man of fashion, took
exception to the prevailing opinion,[12] and in a modern study of the
playwright Richard Barker terms the dialogue "stifling" and Cibber's
point of view that of a social outsider.[13]

Cibber's contemporaries, however, while they often criticized him
for his presumption in hobnobbing with the peers of the realm,
generally conceded that he was thoroughly at home in the world of
the great.[14] And if his dialogue seems a somewhat emasculated tran-
script of the racy talk of this world, Cibber had good reasons for so
altering it. He recognized the social forces that had brought into
power such organizations as the Society for the Reformation of
Manners. At the time of the play's composition Arthur Bedford,
Jeremy Collier's chief disciple, was compiling his own catalogue of the
stage's enormities, and Joseph Addison, the grandfather of Mrs.
Grundy, was at the threshold of his career as an essayist, moralist,
and arbiter of taste. It was not in Cibber's nature to swim against the
tide. If we are to believe a thoroughly hostile critic, John Dennis,
Cibber's own conversation was indecent to the point of blasphemy,[15]
but there is no trace of this in his play. Though he elected to give his
dialogue a high, artificial polish, it is, nonetheless, realistic in other
ways. Lady Betty's torrent of words in her opening scene, as she
describes the latest fashions, has the rush of actual conversation, and
the dialogue throughout is marked by the breaks, hesitations, and
changes of pace that characterize the language of life. Similarly,
Cibber's vocabulary, chastened though it may be, still has consider-
able vitality. The conversation comes alive in the vivid idiom of the
hunting field, the tavern, and the gaming table, and he has the born
writer's instinctive talent for using ordinary words in a fresh and
striking way.

In dramatizing the domestic problems of Sir Charles and Lady
Easy he also makes effective use of everyday materials. Despite the
highly-wrought Steinkirk scene, life, as he sees it, is for the most part
a succession of commonplace moods and incidents. To quote one

[11] Letter of June 14, 1787, to the Countess of Upper Ossory (*Letters*, ed.
Mrs. Paget Toynbee [Oxford, 1903–1905], XIV, 2).
[12] Letter of December 9, 1704, to Joseph Keally (*Works*, ed. Montague
Summers [London, 1923], I, 78).
[13] Richard Barker, *Mr. Cibber of Drury Lane* (New York, 1939), pp. 50–51.
[14] Boswell, *Johnson*, I, 473.
[15] John Dennis, *The Characters and Conduct of Sir John Edgar*, in *Works*, ed.
E. N. Hooker (Baltimore, 1943), II, 188–189.

of his most sympathetic critics, he had an acute sense of "la vie quotidienne." [16]

The theme of his play is thoroughly ordinary, but he treats the problem of marital infidelity with real theatrical originality. A century earlier Thomas Heywood had dramatized an adulterous situation in *A Woman Killed With Kindness*. True to the homiletic tradition, Heywood's outlook was thoroughly male. The transgressor is, naturally, the wife. Her generous-minded husband forgoes revenge but banishes her from his household. Left to herself and her conscience, she has no alternative but to die. Cibber's comedy is an almost exact inversion of Heywood's tragedy. Although Cibber shared Heywood's male prejudices, he recognized the increasing importance of women in the theater on both sides of the footlights. He centers his play on them—there are four women's roles to three for the men—and Lady Easy serves as his focal character. His play is, indeed, a homiletic comedy—A Husband Reclaimed With Kindness.

It is easy to accuse Cibber of meretriciousness and hypocrisy in catering to the public, and there is no doubt that he shared Dr. Johnson's blunt opinion: "The drama's laws the drama's patrons give." It was the secret behind twenty years of successful management of Drury Lane. Cibber was also aware that Jeremy Collier's fulminations against the stage, absurd as they might often be, were not merely the ravings of a fanatic. If in Act V of *The Careless Husband* Cibber laughed at the naiveté of Collier, he was at the same time willing enough to indulge his admirers by including the Steinkirk scene.[17] Chesterfield's observation that hypocrisy is the tribute that vice pays to virtue epitomizes this compliance.

It is at once exasperating and futile to look for consistency in Cibber. In a recent study one of his critics has suggested that he might have been happier had he been born either earlier or later.[18] One might more cogently argue that he is placed exactly right in time. Uncommitted, easy-going, a trimmer by nature, he straddles the Restoration and eighteenth century, and in *The Careless Husband* he reveals to us with particular clarity the clash between the two traditions.

WILLIAM W. APPLETON

Columbia University

[16] F. W. Bateson, *English Comic Drama* (*1700–1750*) (New York, 1963), p. 33.

[17] In Act IV of Cibber's play *The Lady's Last Stake* (1708) Lady Wronglove ridicules the Steinkirk scene.

[18] Bateson, *English Comic Drama*, p. 41.

THE CARELESS HUSBAND

Yet none Sir Fopling him, or him can call,
He's Knight o' th' shire, and represents you all.

Qui Capit, Ille Facit.

Yet . . . all] from Dryden's Epilogue to Etherege's *Man of Mode*.
Qui . . . Facit] If the cap fits, wear it (proverbial).

To the Most Illustrious
JOHN

Duke and Earl of Argyle, Marquis of Lorne, Lord Kintyre Campbell and Lorne, Heritable Master of the Household, Colonel and Captain of her Majesty's troop of the Horse-Guards in Scotland, and Knight of the Most Ancient and Noble Order of St. Andrew.

This play, at last, through many difficulties, has made way to throw itself at your Grace's feet, and considering what well-meant attempts were made to intercept it in its course to so great an honor, I have had reason not to think it entirely successful till (where my ambition always 5 designed it) I found it safe in your protection; which, when several means had failed of making it less worthy of the spleen, ended with the old good nature that was offered to my first play, viz., that it was none of my own. But that's a praise I have indeed some reason to be proud of, since your 10 Grace from evincing circumstances is able to divide the malice from the compliment.

The best critics have long and justly complained that the coarseness of most characters in our late comedies have been unfit entertainments for people of quality, especially 15 the ladies. And therefore I was long in hopes that some able pen (whose expectation did not hang upon the profits of success) would generously attempt to reform the town into

Duke . . . Andrew] *Q 1–2*; Duke of
Argyle *P*.

John . . . Argyle] John Campbell (1678–1734) became Second Duke of Argyle in 1703. He had already distinguished himself as a soldier.

9. *none of my own*] Rumors had circulated widely that *Love's Last Shift* was not by Cibber. Similarly, *The Careless Husband* was persistently attributed to Argyle.

13. *The best critics*] Jeremy Collier's *Short View* (1698) had provoked much discussion. Probably Cibber has in mind the observations of John Dennis and Charles Gildon.

a better taste than the world generally allows 'em. But
nothing of that kind having lately appeared that would   20
give me an opportunity of being wise at another's expense, I
found it impossible any longer to resist the secret temptation
of my vanity, and so even struck the first blow myself. And
the event has now convinced me that whoever sticks closely
to nature can't easily write above the understanding of the   25
galleries, though at the same time he may possibly deserve
applause of the boxes.

The play, before its trial on the stage, was examined by
several people of quality that came into your Grace's
opinion of its being a just, proper and diverting attempt in   30
comedy; but few of 'em carried the compliment beyond their
private approbation, for when I was wishing for a little
farther hope, they stopped short of your Grace's penetration,
and only kindly wished me what they seemed to fear and you
assured me of—a general success.   35

But your Grace has been pleased not only to encourage
me with your judgment, and have likewise, by your
favorable influence in the bounties that were raised me
for the third and sixth day, defended me against any hazards
of an entire disappointment from so bold an undertaking.   40
And therefore, whatever the world may think of me, as one
they call a poet, yet I am confident, as your Grace under-
stands me, I shall not want your belief when I assure you
this dedication is the result of a profound acknowledgement,
an artless inclination, proudly glad and grateful.   45

And if the dialogue of the following scenes flows with
more easy turn of thought and spirit than what I have
usually produced, I shall not yet blame some people for
saying 'tis not my own, unless they knew at the same time
I owe most of it to the many stolen observations I have   50
made from your Grace's manner of conversing.

And if ever the influence of your Grace's more shining
qualities should persuade me to attempt a tragedy, I shall

---

39. *third . . . day*] the author customarily received the profits from the
third and sixth performances.

53. *a tragedy*] Cibber's tragedy *Xerxes* had failed in 1699. He was at this
time probably writing *Perolla and Izadora* (1705), which also failed.

then with the same freedom borrow all the ornamental
virtues of my hero where now I only am indebted for part 55
of the fine gentleman. Greatness of birth and mind, sweetness of temper, flowing from the fixed and native principles
of courage and honor, are beauties that I reserve for a
further opportunity of expressing the zeal and gratitude of,
My Lord, 60
Your Grace's most obedient,
most obliged and humble servant,
COLLEY CIBBER

December 15, 1704

PROLOGUE

Of all the various vices of the age,
And shoals of fools exposed upon the stage,
How few are lashed that call for satire's rage!
What can you think to see our plays so full
Of madmen, coxcombs, and the driveling fool,   5
Of cits, of sharpers, rakes and roaring bullies,
Of Cheats, of cuckolds, aldermen and cullies?
Would not one swear 'twere taken for a rule
That satire's rod in the dramatic school
Was only meant for the incorrigible fool?   10
As if too vice and folly were confined
To the vile scum alone of humankind,
Creatures a muse should scorn; such abject trash
Deserves not satire's but the hangman's lash.
Wretches so far shut out from sense of shame,   15
Newgate or Bedlam only should reclaim,
For satire ne'er was meant to make wild monsters tame.
No, sirs—
    We rather think the persons fit for plays
Are they whose birth and education says   20
They've every help that should improve mankind,
Yet still live slaves to a vile tainted mind;
Such as in wit are often seen t'abound
And yet have some weak part where folly's found,
For follies sprout like weeds, highest in fruitful ground.   25
And 'tis observed, the garden of the mind
To no infestive weed's so much inclined,
As the rank pride that some from affectation find.
A folly too well known to make its court
With most success among the better sort.   30
Such as the persons we today provide,
And nature's fools for once are laid aside.
This is the ground on which our play we build,
But in the structure must to judgment yield,
And where the poet fails in art or care,   35
We beg your wonted mercy to the player.

---

7. *cullies*] dupes.
16. *Newgate or Bedlam*] the prison or the madhouse.

PROLOGUE

Upon the last campaign
Written by a person of quality; designed for the sixth day but not spoken

A paying nation hates the fighting trade,
And lingering war in usual methods made,
When armies walk about from wood to river,
And threescore thousand only get together
To eat and drink, consult, and find the way   5
How without fighting they may earn their pay;
When prudent generals get by safeguard giving, ⎫
An honest, quiet, comfortable living,   ⎬
But never fight it up to a thanksgiving.   ⎭
These manage war with the physician's skill,   10
And use such means as neither cure nor kill.
Like the wise doctors, safe by their degrees,
They give weak doses, but take swinging fees.
The trade continuing, which can never end,
While the sick state has anything to spend.   15
Thanks then to him who strikes at the disease
And bravely tries to set the world at ease,
For if such fighting last but one year more, ⎫
Two Danube victories will quit the score,   ⎬
And soon recruit our almost lavished store. ⎭   20
A happy peace regains our treasure lost,
Our own the glory, and our foes the cost.
　　No favor let the homebred sparks expect
But scorn from men, and from the fair neglect.
Beaux that spend all their time in soft love-making,   25
Those tender souls whose hearts are always aching,

Upon . . . campaign] i.e., Marlborough's Danube Campaign in 1704
against the French and Bavarian forces, which culminated in his victory at
Blenheim.
　a person of quality] perhaps the Duke of Argyle, though he later quarreled
bitterly with Marlborough.
　3. *from . . . river*] from the Black Forest to the Danube.
　13. *swinging*] immense.
　16. *to him*] Marlborough.
　19. *Two Danube victories*] i.e., another Blenheim.

-8-

Shun 'em, ye fair, prevent their am'rous boasting,
Nor poorly yield to idle talk and toasting.
If you have favors which you must bestow,
Give 'em the soldiers, they deserve 'em now, } 30
Who make proud tyrants stoop, should only kneel to you.

   Minerva guides our general to fame,
No cruelties in war affect his name,
Mild in the camp, by no success made vain.
A gentle goddess animates his mind, 35
Bold for his friends, to conquered foes as kind,
Designed by heaven for Anna's happy reign,
Whose generous soul seeks only to restrain
Unbounded tyranny and lawless might,
Revenge oppression and restore the right: 40
War not her choice, but necessary fence,
Truth to promote and humble insolence.
Where'er her influence flies it joy creates,
And peace and safety brings to distant states.
With such success her chief begins his race 45
That his first battle brightly does efface
The tedious labors of our modern wars,
Outdoes at once old soldiers and the tars.
In him no sauntering in the field we find,
No doubt remains where victory inclined. 50
His sword decides, no double praise is given,
Where neither side is pleased, yet both thank heaven.
From war he quickly kingdoms will release,
Rapine and rage soon turn to joy and peace, }
And by destruction make destruction cease. 55

THE PERSONS

LORD MORELOVE	*Mr. Powell*
LORD FOPPINGTON	*Mr. Cibber*
SIR CHARLES EASY	*Mr. Wilks*
LADY BETTY MODISH	*Mrs. Oldfield*
LADY EASY	*Mrs. Knight*
LADY GRAVEAIRS	*Mrs. Moore*
MRS. EDGING, woman to Lady Easy	*Mrs. Lucas*

The Scene: *Windsor*

The Careless Husband

ACT I

Sir Charles Easy's *Lodgings.*
Enter Lady Easy *alone.*

LADY EASY.

Was ever woman's spirit, by an injurious husband, broke
like mine? A vile, licentious man! must he bring home his
follies too? Wrong me with my very servant! Oh, how
tedious a relief is patience! and yet in my condition 'tis the
only remedy, for to reproach him with my wrongs is taking   5
on myself the means of a redress, bidding defiance to his
falsehood, and naturally but provokes him to undo me.
Th'uneasy thought of my continual jealousy may tease him
to a fixed aversion, and hitherto, though he neglects, I cannot think he hates me. —It must be so, since I want power   10
to please him, he never shall upbraid me with an attempt
of making him uneasy. My eyes and tongue shall yet be
blind and silent to my wrongs, nor would I have him think
my virtue could suspect him, till by some gross, apparent
proof of his misdoing he forces me to see—and to forgive it. 15

Enter Edging *hastily.*

EDGING.

Oh, madam!

LADY EASY.

What's the matter?

EDGING.

I have the strangest thing to show your ladyship—such
a discovery—

LADY EASY.

You are resolved to make it without much ceremony, I   20
find. What's the business, pray?

EDGING.

> The business, madam! I have not patience to tell you. I
> am out of breath at the very thoughts on't. I shall not be
> able to speak this half hour.

LADY EASY.

> Not to the purpose, I believe, but methinks you talk   25
> impertinently with a great deal of ease.

EDGING.

> Nay, madam, perhaps not so impertinent as your ladyship
> thinks. There's that will speak to the purpose, I am sure—
> a base man!   *Gives a letter.*

LADY EASY.

> What's this, an open letter? Whence comes it?   30

EDGING.

> Nay, read it, madam, you'll soon guess. If these are the
> tricks of husbands, keep me a maid still, say I.

LADY EASY (*looking on the superscription, aside*).

> "To Sir Charles Easy!" Ha! Too well I know this hateful
> hand. Oh, my heart! But I must veil my jealousy, which
> 'tis not fit this creature should suppose I am acquainted   35
> with. —This direction is to your master. How came you
> by it?

EDGING.

> Why, madam, as my master was lying down, after he came
> in from hunting, he sent me into his dressing room to
> fetch his snuffbox out of his waistcoat pocket, and so, as I   40
> was searching for the box, madam, there I found this wicked
> letter from a mistress, which I had no sooner read but, I
> declare it, my very blood rose at him again; methought I
> could have tore him and her to pieces.

LADY EASY (*aside*).

> Intolerable! This odious thing's jealous of him herself,   45
> and wants me to join with her in a revenge upon him.
> Sure I am fallen indeed! But 'twere to make me lower yet,
> to let her think I understand her.

EDGING.

> Nay, pray, madam, read it; you'll be out of patience at it.

44. tore] *Q 1–2*; torn *P.*

LADY EASY.

You are bold, mistress. Has my indulgence or your master's   50
good humor flattered you into the assurance of reading his
letters?—a liberty I never gave myself. Here, lay it where
you had it immediately. Should he know of your sauciness,
'twould not be my favor could protect you.   *Exit* Lady Easy.

EDGING.

Your favor! Marry come up! Sure I don't depend upon   55
your favor! 'Tis not come to that, I hope. Poor creature,
don't you think I am my master's mistress for nothing. You
shall find, madam, I won't be snapped up as I have been.
Not but it vexes me to think she should not be as uneasy as
I. I am sure he's a base man to me, and I could cry my eyes   60
out that she should not think him as bad to her every jot.
If I am wronged, sure she may very well expect it, that is but
his wife. A conceited thing! She need not be so easy neither.
I am as handsome as she, I hope. —Here's my master. I'll
try whether I am to be huffed by her or no.   *Walks behind.*   65

Enter Sir Charles Easy.

SIR CHARLES EASY.

So! the day is come again. Life but rises to another stage,
and the same dull journey is before us. How like children do
we judge of happiness! When I was stinted in my fortune
almost everything was a pleasure to me because, most things
then being out of my reach, I had always the pleasure of   70
hoping for 'em; now Fortune's in my hand she's as insipid
as an old acquaintance. It's mighty silly, faith. Just the same
thing by my wife too; I am told she's extremely handsome—
nay, and have heard a great many people say she is certainly the best woman in the world—why I don't know but   75
she may [be], yet I could never find that her person or good
qualities gave me any concern. In my eye the woman
has no more charms than her mother.

EDGING.

Humph! He takes no notice of me yet. I'll let him see I can
take as little notice of him.   80

She walks by him gravely, he turns her about and holds her, she struggles.

Pray, sir!

50. or] *Q 1–2*; of *P.*   74. and have] *Q 1–2*; and I have *P.*

SIR CHARLES EASY [*aside*].

A pretty pert air, that. I'll humor it. —What's the matter,
child? Are not you well? Kiss me, hussy.

EDGING.

No, the deuce fetch me if I do.

SIR CHARLES EASY.

Has anything put thee out of humor, love?   85

EDGING.

No, sir, 'tis not worth my being out of humor at—though
if ever you have anything to do with me again I'll be
burned.

SIR CHARLES EASY.

Somebody has belied me to thee.

EDGING.

No, sir, 'tis you have belied yourself to me. Did not I ask   90
you, when you first made a fool of me, if you would be always
constant to me, and did not you say I might be sure you
would? And here, instead of that, you are going on in your
old intrigue with my Lady Graveairs.

SIR CHARLES EASY.

So!   95

EDGING.

Beside, don't you suffer my lady to huff me every day, as if
I were her dog, or had no more concern with you? I declare, I won't bear it, and she shan't think to huff me.
For aught I know I am as agreeable as she, and though she
dares not take any notice of your baseness to her, you shan't 100
think to use me so. And so, pray take your nasty letter.
I know the hand well enough. For my part I won't stay in
the family to be abused at this rate; I that have refused
lords and dukes for your sake. I'd have you know, sir, I have
had as many blue and green ribbons after me, for aught I   105
know, as would have made me a falbala apron.

SIR CHARLES EASY.

"My Lady Graveairs!" "My nasty letter!" and "I won't
stay in the family!"—Death! I'm in a pretty condition.

83. not you] *Q 1–2*; you not *P*.   87. do] *Q 1–2*; say *P*.

105. *blue . . . ribbons*] the Order of the Garter and the Order of the
Thistle.
106. *falbala*] a flounced apron.

What an unlimited privilege has the jade got from being
a whore!   110

EDGING.

I suppose, sir, you think to use everybody as you do your
wife.

SIR CHARLES EASY.

My wife, ha! Come hither, Mrs. Edging. Hark you, drab.

Seizing her by the shoulder.

EDGING.

Oh!

SIR CHARLES EASY.

When you speak of my wife you are to say "your lady," and 115
you are never to speak of your lady to me in any regard of
her being my wife, for look you, child, you are not her
strumpet but mine, therefore I only give you leave to be
saucy with me; in the next place, you are never to suppose
there is any such person as my Lady Graveairs; and lastly, 120
my pretty one, how came you by this letter?

EDGING.

It's no matter, perhaps.

SIR CHARLES EASY.

Ay, but if you should not tell me quickly, how are you
sure I won't take a great piece of flesh out of your shoulder?
—my dear!   *Shakes her.* 125

EDGING.

O lud! O lud! I will tell you, sir.

SIR CHARLES EASY.

Quickly, then.   *Again.*

EDGING.

Oh! I took it out of your pocket, sir.

SIR CHARLES EASY.

When?

EDGING.

Oh! this morning, when you sent me for your snuffbox.   130

SIR CHARLES EASY.

And your ladyship's pretty curiosity has looked it over, I
presume? Ha!   *Again.*

EDGING.

O lud! dear sir, don't be angry; indeed I'll never touch
one again.

SIR CHARLES EASY.

I don't believe you will, and I'll tell you how you shall be 135
sure you never will.

EDGING.

Yes, sir.

SIR CHARLES EASY.

By steadfastly believing that the next time you offer it,
you will have your pretty white neck twisted behind you.

EDGING.

Yes, sir.   *Curtsying.* 140

SIR CHARLES EASY.

And you will be sure to remember everything I have said
to you?

EDGING.

Yes, sir.

SIR CHARLES EASY.

And now, child, I was not angry with your person, but
your follies, which, since I find you are a little sensible of, 145
don't be wholly discouraged, for I believe I—I shall have
occasion for you again.

EDGING.

Yes, sir.

SIR CHARLES EASY.

In the meantime let me hear no more of your lady, child.

EDGING.

No, sir.   150

SIR CHARLES EASY.

Here she comes. Begone.

EDGING.

Yes, sir.— [*Aside.*] Oh! I was never so frightened in my
life.   *Exit* Edging.

SIR CHARLES EASY.

So! Good discipline makes good soldiers. It often puzzles
me to think, from my own carelessness and my wife's con- 155
tinual good humor, whether she really knows anything of
the strength of my forces. I'll sift her a little.

Enter Lady Easy.

My dear, how do you do? You are dressed very early today;
are you going out?

-16-

LADY EASY.

Only to church, my dear.   160

SIR CHARLES EASY.

Is it so late then?

LADY EASY.

The bell has just rung.

SIR CHARLES EASY.

Well, child, how does the Windsor air agree with you? Do
you find yourself any better yet? or have you a mind to go to
London again?   165

LADY EASY.

No, indeed, my dear; the air's so very pleasant that if it were
a place of less company I could be content to end my days
here.

SIR CHARLES EASY.

Prithee, my dear, what sort of company would most please
you?   170

LADY EASY.

When business would permit it, yours; and in your absence
a sincere friend that were truly happy in an honest husband,
to sit a cheerful hour and talk in mutual praise of our
condition.

SIR CHARLES EASY.

Are you then really very happy, my dear?   175

LADY EASY.

Why should you question it?   *Smiling on him.*

SIR CHARLES EASY.

Because I fancy I am not so good to you as I should be.

LADY EASY.

Pshaw!

SIR CHARLES EASY.

Nay, the deuce take me if I don't really confess myself so
bad that I have often wondered how any woman of your 180
sense, rank, and person could think it worth her while to
have so many useless good qualities.

LADY EASY.

Fie, my dear!

SIR CHARLES EASY.

By my soul, I'm serious.

LADY EASY.

I can't boast of my good qualities, nor if I could, do I believe 185
you think 'em useless.

SIR CHARLES EASY.

Nay, I submit to you, don't you find 'em so? Do you perceive that I am one tittle the better husband for your
being so good a wife?

LADY EASY.

Pshaw! You jest with me.   190

SIR CHARLES EASY.

I don't really. Tell me truly, was you never jealous of me?

LADY EASY.

Did I ever give you any sign of it?

SIR CHARLES EASY.

Um—that's true—but do you really think I never gave you
occasion?

LADY EASY.

That's an odd question; but suppose you had?   195

SIR CHARLES EASY.

Why then, what good has your virtue done you, since all
the good qualities of it could not keep me to yourself?

LADY EASY.

What occasion have you given me to suppose I have not
kept you to myself?

SIR CHARLES EASY.

I given you occasion? Fie! my dear, you may be sure I—I 200
—look you, that is not the thing, but still a—(Death! what a
blunder have I made)—a still, I say, madam, you shan't
make me believe you have never been jealous of me, not that
you ever had any real cause, but I know women of your
principles have more pride than those that have no princi- 205
ples at all, and where there is pride there must be some
jealousy—so that if you are jealous, my dear, you know you
wrong me and—

LADY EASY.

Why then upon my word, my dear, I don't know that ever
I wronged you that way in my life.   210

191. I . . . . Tell] *Q 1–2*; Upon my
life, I don't. Tell *P.*

SIR CHARLES EASY.

But suppose I had given you a real cause to be jealous,
how would you do then?

LADY EASY.

It must be a very substantial one that makes me jealous.

SIR CHARLES EASY.

Say it were a substantial one; suppose now I were well
with a woman of your own acquaintance, that under pre-   215
tense of frequent visits to you, should only come to carry
on an affair with me. Suppose now my Lady Graveairs and
I were great—

LADY EASY (*aside*).

Would I could not suppose it.

SIR CHARLES EASY (*aside*).

If I come off here I believe I am pretty safe. —Suppose, I   220
say, my lady and I were so very familiar that not only
yourself, but half the town should see it?

LADY EASY.

Then I should cry myself sick in some dark closet, and
forget my tears when you spoke kindly to me.

SIR CHARLES EASY (*aside*).

The most convenient piece of virtue, sure, that ever wife was   225
mistress of.

LADY EASY.

But pray, my dear, did you ever think that I had any ill
thoughts of my Lady Graveairs?

SIR CHARLES EASY.

Oh fie, child. Only you know she and I used to be a little
free sometimes, so I had a mind to see if you thought   230
there was any harm in it. But since I find you very easy, I
think myself obliged to tell you that upon my soul, my dear,
I have so little regard to her person that the deuce take me if
I would not as soon have an affair with thy own woman.

LADY EASY.

Indeed, my dear, I should as soon suspect you with one as   235
t'other.

SIR CHARLES EASY.

Poor dear—shouldst thou? Give me a kiss!

---

218. *great*] intimate.

LADY EASY.

Pshaw! You don't care to kiss me.

SIR CHARLES EASY.

By my soul, I do. I wish I may die if I don't think you a
very fine woman.   240

LADY EASY.

I only wish you would think me a good wife. (*Kisses her.*)
But pray, my dear, what has made you so strangely
inquisitive?

SIR CHARLES EASY.

Inquisitive? Why—a—nay, I don't know, one's always
saying one foolish thing or another—*toll le roll.* (*Sings and* 245
talks.)   My dear, what, are we never to have any ball here?
Toll le roll. I fancy I could recover my dancing again, if I
would but practise. *Toll loll loll!*

LADY EASY [*aside*].

This excess of carelessness to me excuses half his vices, if I
can make him once think seriously. Time yet may be my 250
friend.

Enter a Servant.

SERVANT.

Sir, my Lord Morelove gives his service—

SIR CHARLES EASY.

Lord Morelove! Where is he?

SERVANT.

At the chocolate-house. He called me to him as I went by
and bid me tell your honor he'll wait upon you presently. 255

LADY EASY.

I thought you had not expected him here again this
season, my dear.

SIR CHARLES EASY.

I thought so too, but you see there's no depending upon
the resolution of a man that's in love.

LADY EASY.

Is there a chair?   260

SERVANT.

Yes, madam.   *Exit* Servant.

244. nay] *Q 1–2; om. P.*

LADY EASY.

I suppose Lady Betty Modish has drawn him hither.

SIR CHARLES EASY.

Ay, poor soul, for all his bravery, I am afraid so.

LADY EASY.

Well, my dear, I han't time to ask my lord how he does
now; you'll excuse me to him, but I hope you'll make him 265
dine with us.

SIR CHARLES EASY.

I'll ask him; if you see Lady Betty at prayers make her
dine too, but don't take any notice of my lord's being in
town.

LADY EASY.

Very well. If I should not meet her there, I'll call at her 270
lodgings.

SIR CHARLES EASY.

Do so.

LADY EASY.

My dear, your servant.

SIR CHARLES EASY.

My dear, I'm yours.   *Exit* Lady Easy.
Well, one way or other this woman will certainly bring 275
about her business with me at last; for though she can't make
me happy in her own person, she lets me be so intolerably
easy with the women that can that she has at least brought
me into a fair way of being as weary of them too.

Enter Servant *and* Lord Morelove.

SERVANT.

Sir, my lord's come.   280

LORD MORELOVE.

Dear Charles!

SIR CHARLES EASY.

My dear lord! This is an happiness undreamed of. I little
thought to have seen you at Windsor again this season.
I concluded, of course, that books and solitude had secured
you till winter.   285

272.] *Q 1–2 include a S.D. (Re-
enter the Servant); om. P.*

LORD MORELOVE.

Nay, I did not think of coming myself, but I found myself not very well in London, so I thought—a—little hunting and this air—

SIR CHARLES EASY.

Ha, ha, ha!

LORD MORELOVE.

What do you laugh at? 290

SIR CHARLES EASY.

Only because you should not go on with your story. If you did but see how sillily a man fumbles for an excuse when he's a little ashamed of being in love, you would not wonder what I laugh at. Ha, ha!

LORD MORELOVE.

Thou art a very happy fellow—nothing touches thee— 295 always easy. Then you conclude I follow Lady Betty again?

SIR CHARLES EASY.

Yes, faith, do I, and to make you easy, my lord, I cannot see why a man that can ride fifty miles after a poor stag should be ashamed of running twenty in chase of a fine woman that, in all probability, will make him so much the 300 better sport too.   *Embracing.*

LORD MORELOVE.

Dear Charles, don't flatter my distemper. I own I still follow her. Do you think her charms have power to excuse me to the world?

SIR CHARLES EASY.

Ay! ay! a fine woman's an excuse for anything. 305

LORD MORELOVE.

You take a great deal of pains to give me hope, but I can't believe she has the least degree of inclination for me.

SIR CHARLES EASY.

I don't know that. I am sure her pride likes you, and that's generally your fine lady's darling passion.

305. anything] *Q 1–2;* anything; and the scandal of being her jest is a jest itself; we are all forced to be their fools before we can be their favorites. *P.*

306. You take] *Q 1–2;* You are willing to take *P.*
308. I am] *Q 1–2;* I'm *P.*

LORD MORELOVE.

Do you suppose if I could grow indifferent it would touch 310
her?

SIR CHARLES EASY.

Sting her to the heart. Will you take my advice?

LORD MORELOVE.

I have no relief but that. Had I not thee now and then to
talk an hour, my life were insupportable.

SIR CHARLES EASY.

I am sorry for that, my lord, but mind what I say to you. 315
But hold! First let me know the particulars of your quarrel
with her.

LORD MORELOVE.

Why, about three weeks ago, when I was last here at
Windsor, she had for some days treated me with a little
more reserve, and another with more freedom than I found 320
myself easy at.

SIR CHARLES EASY.

Who was that other?

LORD MORELOVE.

One of my Lord Foppington's gang, the pert coxcomb that's
just come to a small estate and a great periwig—he that
sings himself among the women—what d'ye call him? He 325
won't speak to a gentleman when a lord's in company. You
always see him with a cane dangling at his button, his breast
open, no gloves, one eye tucked under his hat, and a tooth-
pick—*Startup*! That's his name.

SIR CHARLES EASY.

Oh! I have met him in a visit—but pray go on.   330

LORD MORELOVE.

So, disputing with her about the conduct of women, I took
the liberty to tell her how far I thought she erred in hers;
she told me I was rude, and that she would never believe any
man could love a woman that thought her in the wrong in
anything she had a mind to, at least if he dared to tell her 335
so. This provoked me into her whole character, with as

314. were] *Q 2, P*; we *Q 1*.   326. gentleman] *Q 1-2*; commoner
316. your] *Q 1-2*; your late *P*.   *P*.

much spite and civil malice as I have seen her bestow upon
a woman of true beauty when the men first toasted her; so,
in the middle of my wisdom, she told me she desired to be
alone, that I would take my odious proud heart along with 340
me and trouble her no more. I bowed very low, and, as I left
the room, vowed I never would, and that my proud heart
should never be humbled by the outside of a fine woman.
About an hour after I whipped into my chaise for London,
and have never seen her since.   345

SIR CHARLES EASY.

Very well, and how did you find your proud heart by that
time you got to Hounslow?

LORD MORELOVE.

I am almost ashamed to tell you. I found her so much in
the right that I cursed my pride for contradicting her at all,
and began to think that no woman could be in the wrong to 350
a man that she had in her power.

SIR CHARLES EASY.

Ha, ha! Well, I'll tell you what you shall do. You can see
her without trembling, I hope?

LORD MORELOVE.

Not if she receives me well.

SIR CHARLES EASY.

If she receives you well, you will have no occasion for 355
what I am going to say to you. First, you shall dine with
her.

LORD MORELOVE.

How? where? when?

SIR CHARLES EASY.

Here! here! at two o'clock.

LORD MORELOVE.

Dear Charles!   360

SIR CHARLES EASY.

My wife's gone to invite her. When you see her first, be
neither too humble nor too stubborn; let her see by the ease
in your behavior you are still pleased in being near her

350. think   that]   *Q 1–2*;   think,
according to her maxim, that *P*.

347. *Hounslow*] midway point between Windsor and London.

while she is upon reasonable terms with you. This will either
open the door of an *éclaircissement*, or quite shut it against you. 365
If she is still resolved to keep you out—

LORD MORELOVE.

Nay, if she insults me then, perhaps I may recover pride
enough to rally her by an overacted submission.

SIR CHARLES EASY.

Why, you improve, my lord. This is the very thing I was
going to propose to you.   370

LORD MORELOVE.

Was it, faith! Hark you, dare you stand by me?

SIR CHARLES EASY.

Dare I? Ay, to my last drop of assurance, against all the insolent airs of the proudest beauty in Christendom.

LORD MORELOVE.

Nay, then, defiance to her! We two—! Thou hast inspired
me. I find myself as valiant as a flattered coward.   375

SIR CHARLES EASY.

Courage, my lord. I'll warrant we beat her.

LORD MORELOVE.

My blood stirs at the very thought on't. I long to be
engaged.

SIR CHARLES EASY.

She'll certainly give ground when she once sees you are
thoroughly provoked.   380

LORD MORELOVE.

Dear Charles, thou art a friend indeed.

Enter a Servant.

SERVANT.

Sir, my Lord Foppington gives his service, and if your
honor's at leisure, he'll wait on you as soon as he's dressed.

LORD MORELOVE.

Lord Foppington! Is he is town?

SIR CHARLES EASY.

Yes, I heard last night he was come. Give my service to 385
his lordship and tell him I shall be glad he'll do me the honor

365–366. you. If] *Q 1–2*; you—and if *P.*

---

365. *éclaircissement*] understanding.

of his company here at dinner.   *Exit* Servant.
We may have occasion for him in our design upon Lady
Betty.

LORD MORELOVE.

What use can we make of him? 390

SIR CHARLES EASY.

We'll see when he comes. At least there's no danger in him;
not but I suppose you know he's your rival.

LORD MORELOVE.

Pshaw! A coxcomb!

SIR CHARLES EASY.

Nay, don't despise him neither. He's able to give you
advice, for though he's in love with the same woman, yet to 395
him she has not charms enough to give a minute's pain.

LORD MORELOVE.

Prithee, what sense has he of love?

SIR CHARLES EASY.

Faith, very near as much as a man of sense ought to have.
I grant you he knows not how to value a woman truly
deserving, but he has a pretty just esteem for most ladies 400
about town.

LORD MORELOVE.

That he follows, I grant you, for he seldom visits any of
extraordinary reputation.

SIR CHARLES EASY.

Have a care. I have seen him at Lady Betty Modish's.

LORD MORELOVE.

To be laughed at. 405

SIR CHARLES EASY.

Don't be too confident of that. The women now begin to
laugh *with* him, not *at* him, for he really sometimes rallies
his own humor with so much ease and pleasantry that a great
many women begin to think he has no follies at all, and those
he has have been as much owing to his youth and a great 410
estate as want of natural wit. 'Tis true, he's often a bubble
to his pleasures, but he has always been wisely vain enough
to keep himself from being too much the ladies' humble
servant in love.

LORD MORELOVE.

There indeed I almost envy him. 415

SIR CHARLES EASY.

The easiness of his opinion upon the sex will go near to pique you. We must have him.

LORD MORELOVE.

As you please. But what shall we do with ourselves till dinner?

SIR CHARLES EASY.

What think you of a party at piquet?   420

LORD MORELOVE.

Oh, you are too hard for me.

SIR CHARLES EASY.

Fie! fie! what, when you play with his grace?

LORD MORELOVE.

Upon my soul, he gives me three points.

SIR CHARLES EASY.

Does he? Why then you shall give me but two. —[*Calls to a servant.*] Here, fellow, get cards. *Allons.*   *Exeunt.* 425

---

420. *piquet*] card game for two.

ACT II

The scene, Lady Betty Modish's *Lodgings.*
Enter Lady Betty *and* Lady Easy, *meeting.*

LADY BETTY MODISH.

Oh, my dear! I am overjoyed to see you! I am strangely
happy today; I have just received my new scarf from
London, and you are most critically come to give me your
opinion of it.

LADY EASY.

Oh, your servant, madam! I am a very indifferent judge, 5
you know. What, is it with sleeves?

LADY BETTY MODISH.

Oh, 'tis impossible to tell you what it is. 'Tis all extrav-
agance both in mode and fancy. My dear, I believe
there's six thousand yards of edging in it, then such an
enchanting slope from the elbow, something so new, so 10
lively, so noble, so coquet and charming—but you shall see it,
my dear.

LADY EASY.

Indeed I won't, my dear; I am resolved to mortify you for
being so wrongly fond of a trifle.

LADY BETTY MODISH.

Nay, now, my dear, you are ill-natured. 15

LADY EASY.

Why truly, I am half angry to see a woman of your sense
so warmly concerned in the care of her outside; for when
we have taken our best pains about it, 'tis the beauty of the
mind alone that gives us lasting value.

LADY BETTY MODISH.

Ah, my dear, my dear! you have been a married woman to 20
a fine purpose indeed, that know so little of the taste of
mankind. Take my word, a new fashion upon a fine woman
is often a greater proof of her value than you are aware of.

LADY EASY.

That I can't comprehend, for you see among the men
nothing's more ridiculous than a new fashion. Those 25
of the first sense are always the last that come into 'em.

16. I am] *Q 1;* I'm *Q 2, P.*

LADY BETTY MODISH.

That is because the only merit of a man is his sense, but
doubtless the greatest value of a woman is her beauty. An
homely woman at the head of a fashion would not be allowed
in it by the men, and consequently not followed by the   30
women, so that to be successful in one's fancy is an evident
sign of one's being admired, and I always take admiration
for the best proof of beauty, and beauty certainly is the
source of power, as power in all creatures is the height of
happiness.   35

LADY EASY.

At this rate you would rather be thought beautiful than
good?

LADY BETTY MODISH.

As I had rather command than obey. The wisest homely
woman can't make a man of sense a fool, but the veriest
fool of a beauty shall make an ass of a statesman; so that, 40
in short, I can't see a woman of spirit has any business in
this world but to dress—and make the men like her.

LADY EASY.

Do you suppose this is a principle the men of sense will
admire you for?

LADY BETTY MODISH.

I do suppose that when I suffer any man to like my person 45
he shan't dare to find fault with my principle.

LADY EASY.

But men of sense are not so easily humbled.

LADY BETTY MODISH.

The easiest of any. One has ten thousand times the trouble
with a coxcomb.

LADY EASY.

Nay, that may be, for I have seen you throw away more   50
good humor in hopes of a *tendresse* from my Lord Foppington, who loves all women alike, than would have made my
Lord Morelove perfectly happy, who loves only you.

LADY BETTY MODISH.

The men of sense, my dear, make the best fools in the
world. Their sincerity and good breeding throws 'em so   55

36. would] *Q 1–2*; had *P.*   37. good?] *Q 1*; good; *Q 2*; good. *P.*

entirely into one's power, and gives one such an agreeable thirst of using 'em ill, to show that power—'tis impossible not to quench it.

LADY EASY.

But methinks my Lord Morelove's manner to you might move any woman to a kinder sense of his merit.   60

LADY BETTY MODISH.

Ay! But would it not be hard, my dear, for a poor weak woman to have a man of his quality and reputation in her power and not to let the world see him there? Would any creature sit new-dressed all day in her closet? Could you bear to have a sweet-fancied suit and never show it at the   65 play or the drawing room?

LADY EASY.

But one would not ride in't, methinks, or harass it out when there's no occasion.

LADY BETTY MODISH.

Pooh! My Lord Morelove's a mere Indian damask—one can't wear him out; o' my conscience, I must give him   70 to my woman at last; I begin to be known by him. Had not I best leave him off, my dear? For (poor soul) I believe I have a little fretted him of late.

LADY EASY.

Now 'tis to me amazing how a man of his spirit can bear to be used like a dog for four or five years together— but   75 nothing's a wonder in love. Yet pray, when you found you could not like him at first, why did you ever encourage him?

LADY BETTY MODISH.

Why, what would you have one do? For my part, I could no more choose a man by my eye than a shoe; one must   80 draw 'em on a little to see if they are right to one's foot.

LADY EASY.

But I'd no more fool on with a man I could not like than I'd wear a shoe that pinched me.

LADY BETTY MODISH.

Ay, but then a poor wretch tells one he'll widen 'em, or

63. to] *Q 1*; *om. Q 2, P.*   67. in't] *Q 1*; in it *Q 2, P.*

69. *Indian damask*] inexpensive wool or cloth imitation of Damascus silk.

do anything, and is so civil and silly, that one does not know   85
how to turn such a trifle as a pair of shoes or an heart upon
a fellow's hands again.

LADY EASY.

Well! I confess you are very happily distinguished amongst
most women of fortune to have a man of my Lord Morelove's
sense and quality so long and honorably in love with you,   90
for nowadays one hardly ever hears of such a thing as a man
of quality in love with the women he would marry. To be
in love now is only having a design upon a woman, a modish
way of declaring war against her virtue, which they generally attack first by toasting up her vanity.   95

LADY BETTY MODISH.

Ay, but the world knows that is not the case between my
lord and me.

LADY EASY.

Therefore I think you happy.

LADY BETTY MODISH.

Now I don't see it; I'll swear I'm better pleased to know
there are a great many foolish fellows of quality that take 100
occasion to toast me frequently.

LADY EASY.

I vow I should not thank any gentleman for toasting me,
and I have often wondered how a woman of your spirit
could bear a great many other freedoms I have seen some
men take with you.   105

LADY BETTY MODISH.

As how, my dear? Come, prithee be free with me, for you
must know I love dearly to hear my faults. Who is't you
have observed to be too free with me?

LADY EASY.

Why, there's my Lord Foppington. Could any woman but
you bear to see him with a respectful fleer stare full in her 110
face, draw up his breath and cry, "Gad, you're handsome!"

LADY BETTY MODISH.

My dear, fine fruit will have flies about it, but, poor things,
they do it no harm; for, if you observe, people are always

113. always] *Q 1–2*; generally *P*.

110. *fleer*] mocking look or deceitful grin.

most apt to choose that that the flies have been busy with—
ha, ha!   115

LADY EASY.

Thou art a strange, giddy creature.

LADY BETTY MODISH.

That may be from so much circulation of thought, my dear.

LADY EASY.

But my Lord Foppington's married, and one would not fool
with him for his lady's sake. It may make her uneasy and—

LADY BETTY MODISH.

Poor creature, her pride indeed makes her carry it off without 120
taking any notice of it to me, though I know she hates me
in her heart, and I can't endure malicious people, so I
used to dine there once a week purely to give her disorder.
If you had but seen her when my lord and I fooled a
little, the creature looked so ugly.   125

LADY EASY.

But I should not think my reputation safe; my Lord
Foppington's a man that talks often of his amours, but
seldom speaks of favors that are refused him.

LADY BETTY MODISH.

Pshaw! Will anything a man says make a woman less agreeable? Will his talking spoil one's complexion, or put one's 130
hair out of order? And for reputation—look you, my dear,
take it for a rule that as amongst the lower rank of people
no woman wants beauty that has fortune, so amongst people
of fortune no woman wants virtue that has beauty. But an
estate and beauty joined is of an unlimited—nay, a power 135
pontifical, makes one not only absolute, but infallible. A
fine woman's never in the wrong, or if we were, 'tis not the
strength of a poor creature's reason that can unfetter him.
Oh, how I love to hear a wretch curse himself for loving on,
or now and then coming out with a   140

          Yet, for the plague of human race,
          This devil has an angel's face.

LADY EASY.

At this rate I don't see you allow reputation to be at all
essential to a fine woman.

LADY BETTY MODISH.

Just as much as honor to a great man. Power always is above 145 scandal. Don't you hear people say the King of France owes most of his conquests to breaking his word? And would not the confederates have a fine time on't if they were only to go to war with reproaches? Indeed, my dear, that jewel reputation is but a very fanciful business. One 150 shall not see an homely creature in town but wears it in her mouth as monstrously as the Indians do bobs at their lips, and it really becomes 'em just alike.

LADY EASY.

Have a care, my dear, of being too eagerly fond of power, for nothing is more ridiculous than the fall of pride, and 155 woman's pride at best may be suspected to be more a distrust than a real contempt of mankind. For when we have said all we can, a deserving husband is certainly our best happiness, and I don't question but my Lord Morelove's merit, in a little time, will make you think so too, for what- 160 ever airs you give yourself to the world, I am sure your heart don't want good nature.

LADY BETTY MODISH.

You are mistaken. I am very ill-natured, though your good humor won't let you see it.

LADY EASY.

Then to give me proof on't, let me see you refuse to go 165 immediately and dine with me, after I have promised Sir Charles to bring you.

LADY BETTY MODISH.

Pray don't ask me.

LADY EASY.

Why?

LADY BETTY MODISH.

Because, to let you see I hate good nature, I'll go without 170 asking, that you mayn't have the malice to say I did you a favor.

154–155. being . . . for]   *Q 1–2*;
trusting too far to power alone for *P*.

---

147. *breaking his word*] allusion to Louis XIV's violation of articles after the Peace of Ryswick (1697).
148. *confederates*] England, Holland, Denmark, Portugal, Austria, and some of the German states.
152. *bobs*] pendants.

LADY EASY.

Thou art a mad creature.   *Exeunt.*

[II.ii]   *The scene changes to* Sir Charles's *lodgings.*
                 Lord Morelove *and* Sir Charles *at piquet.*

SIR CHARLES EASY.

Come, my lord, one single game for the *tout*, and so have
done.

LORD MORELOVE.

No, hang 'em, I have enough of 'em. Ill cards are the
dullest company in the world. How much is it?

SIR CHARLES EASY.

Three parties.   5

LORD MORELOVE.

Fifteen pound—very well.

While Lord Morelove *counts out his money a Servant gives* Sir Charles *a
letter, which he reads to himself.*

SIR CHARLES EASY (*to the Servant*).

Give my service, say I have company dines with me. If I have
time I'll call there in the afternoon—ha, ha, ha!

                                                    Exit Servant.

LORD MORELOVE.

What's the matter?

SIR CHARLES EASY.

The old affair—my Lady Graveairs.   10

LORD MORELOVE.

Oh! Prithee, how does that go forward? Here—

                                              Paying the money.

SIR CHARLES EASY.

As agreeably as a chancery suit, for now it's come to the
intolerable plague of my not being able to get rid on't, as
you may see.   *Giving the letter.*

LORD MORELOVE (*reads*).

"Your behavior since I came to Windsor has convinced   15
me of your villainy, without my being surprised or angry

173. S.D.] Q 1–2; *Exeunt arm in arm.*   11. forward] Q 1–2; on P.
P.   11.1.] P; om. Q 1–2.

_____

1. *tout*] all; i.e., one game to decide the outcome.
5. *parties*] sets of five games.

at it. I desire you would let me see you at my lodgings immediately, where I shall have a better opportunity to satisfy you that I never can, or positively will be, as I have been, Yours." —A very whimsical letter! Faith, I think she 20
has hard luck with you. If a man were obliged to have a mistress, her person and condition seem to be cut out for the ease of a lover, for she's a young, handsome, wild, well-jointed widow. But what's your quarrel?

SIR CHARLES EASY.

Nothing. She sees the coolness happens to be first of my 25
side, and her business with me now, I suppose, is to convince me how heartily she's vexed that she was not beforehand with me.

LORD MORELOVE.

Her pride and your indifference must occasion a pleasant scene, sure. What do you intend to do?   30

SIR CHARLES EASY.

Treat her with a cool, familiar air, till I pique her to forbid me her sight, and then take her at her word.

LORD MORELOVE.

Very gallant and provoking.

Enter a Servant.

SERVANT.

Sir, my Lord Foppington's come.   *Exit.*

SIR CHARLES EASY.

Oh! Now, my lord, if you have a mind to be let into the 35
mystery of making love without pain, here's one that's a master of the art and shall declaim to you.

Enter Lord Foppington.

My dear Lord Foppington!

LORD FOPPINGTON.

My dear agreeable! *Que je t'embrasse! Pardi! Il y a cent ans*

19. satisfy] *Q 1–2*; convince *P.*   25. of] *Q 1–2*; on *P.*
20. Yours] *Q 1–2*; Yours etc. *P.*   34. Foppington's come.] *Q 1–2*;
23–24. well-jointed] *Q 1–2*; well-   Foppington. *P.*
jointured *P.*

39–40. *Que . . . vu*] Let me embrace you. Gad, it's a hundred years since I've seen you.

que je ne t'ai vu. My lord, I am your lordship's most obedient   40
humble servant.

LORD MORELOVE.

My lord, I kiss your hand. I hope we shall have you here
some time. You seem to have laid in a stock of health to be
in at the diversions of the place. You look extremely well.

LORD FOPPINGTON.

To see one's friends look so, my lord, may easily give a   45
vermeil to one's complexion.

SIR CHARLES EASY.

Lovers in hope, my lord, always have a visible *brillant* in
their eyes and air.

LORD FOPPINGTON.

What dost thou mean, Charles?

SIR CHARLES EASY.

Come, come, my lord, confess what really brought you to   50
Windsor, now you have no business here.

LORD FOPPINGTON.

Why, two hours and six of the best nags in Christendom,
or the devil drive me.

LORD MORELOVE.

You make haste, my lord.

LORD FOPPINGTON.

My lord, I always fly when I pursue. But they are well kept   55
indeed. I love to have creatures go as I bid 'em. You
have seen 'em, Charles, but so has all the world. Foppington's long-tails are known in every road in England.

SIR CHARLES EASY.

Well, my lord, but how came they to bring you this road?
You don't use to take these irregular jaunts without some   60
design in your head of having more than nothing to do.

LORD FOPPINGTON.

Pshaw! Prithee, pox! Charles, thou knowest I am a fellow
sans conséquence, be where I will.

43. a] *P*; *om. Q 1–2.*   51. here] *Q 1–2*; there *P*.
45. my lord] *Q 1–2*; *om. P.*   62. prithee, pox] *Q 1–2*; pox!
50. my lord] *Q 1–2*; *om. P.*   prithee *P*.

46. *vermeil*] high color.
47. *brillant*] sparkle.

SIR CHARLES EASY.

Nay, nay, we must have it. Come, come, your real business
here?   65

LORD FOPPINGTON.

Why then, *entre nous*, there is a certain *fille de joie* about the
court here that loves winning at cards better than all the
fine things I have been able to say to her, so I have brought
an odd thousand pound bill in my pocket that I design *tête-
à-tête* to play off with her at piquet—and now the business   70
is out.

SIR CHARLES EASY.

Ah! and a very good business, too, my lord.

LORD FOPPINGTON.

If it be well done, Charles.

SIR CHARLES EASY.

That's as you manage your cards, my lord.

LORD MORELOVE.

This must be a woman of some consequence, by the value   75
you set on her favors.

SIR CHARLES EASY.

Pshaw! Nothing's above the price of a fine woman.

LORD FOPPINGTON.

Nay, look you, gentlemen, the price may not happen to be
altogether so high neither, for, all this while, I fancy I know
enough of the game to make it but an even bet that I get   80
her for nothing.

LORD MORELOVE.

How so, my lord?

LORD FOPPINGTON.

Because, if she happens to lose a good sum to me, I shall
buy her with her own money.

LORD MORELOVE.

That's new, I confess.   85

---

64. Nay . . . your] *Q 1–2*; Nay, nay
this is too much among friends, my
lord. Come, come we must have it:
your *P.*
69. pound] *Q 1–2*; *om. P.*
70. piquet—and] *Q 1–2*; piquet or
so and *P.*

75. some] *Q 1–2*; *om. P.*
77. Pshaw!] *Q 1–2*; Oh! *P.*
79. all this while] *Q 1–2*; *om. P.*
80. that] *Q 1–2*; *om. P.*
83. happens] *Q 1–2*; happen *P.*

LORD FOPPINGTON.

You know, Charles, 'tis not impossible but I may be five
hundred pound deep with her, then bills may fall short,
and the devil's in't if I want assurance to ask her to pay me
some way or other.

SIR CHARLES EASY.

And a man must be a churl indeed that won't take a lady's   90
personal security—ha, ha, ha!

LORD FOPPINGTON.

Heh, heh, heh! Thou art a devil, Charles.

LORD MORELOVE (*aside*).

Death! How happy is this coxcomb!

LORD FOPPINGTON.

But to tell you the truth, gentlemen, I had another pressing
temptation that brought me hither, which was—my wife.   95

LORD MORELOVE.

That's kind, indeed. My lady has been here this fortnight.
She'll be glad to see you.

LORD FOPPINGTON.

That I don't know, for I design this afternoon to send her to
London.

LORD MORELOVE.

What! The same day you come, my lord? That would be   100
cruel.

LORD FOPPINGTON.

Ay, but it will be mighty convenient, for she is positively
of no manner of use in my amours.

LORD MORELOVE.

That's your fault. The town thinks her a very deserving
woman.   105

LORD FOPPINGTON.

If she were a woman of the town, perhaps I should think
so too, but she happens to be my wife, and when a wife
is once given to deserve more than her husband can pay,
in my mind she has no merit at all.

LORD MORELOVE.

She's extremely well bred, and of a very prudent conduct.   110

96. fortnight] *Q 1–2*; month *P*.   108. husband] *Q 1–2*; husband's
                                            inclinations *P*.

LORD FOPPINGTON.

Um—ay, the woman's proud enough.

LORD MORELOVE.

Add to this, all the world allows her handsome.

LORD FOPPINGTON.

The world's very civil, my lord, and I should take it as a favor done to me if they could find an expedient to unmarry the poor woman from the only man in the world that can't 115 think her handsome.

LORD MORELOVE.

I believe there are a great many in the world that are sorry 'tis not in their power to unmarry her.

LORD FOPPINGTON.

I am a great many in the world's very humble servant, and whenever they find 'tis in their power, their high and 120 mighty wisdoms may command me at a quarter of an hour's warning.

LORD MORELOVE.

Pray, my lord, what did you marry for?

LORD FOPPINGTON.

To pay my debts at play and disinherit my younger brother. 125

LORD MORELOVE.

But there are some things due to a wife.

LORD FOPPINGTON.

And there are some debts I don't care to pay—to both [of] which I plead husband and my lord.

LORD MORELOVE.

If I should do so, I should expect to have my own coach stopped in the street, and to meet my wife with the windows 130 up in a hackney.

LORD FOPPINGTON.

Then would I put in bail, and order a separate maintenance.

LORD MORELOVE.

So pay double the sum of the debt, and be married for nothing.

LORD FOPPINGTON.

Now I think deferring a dun and getting rid of one's wife 135

112. Add] *P*; And *Q 1–2*.   113. very] *Q 1–2*; extremely *P*.

are two [of] the most agreeable sweets in the liberties of an
English subject.

LORD MORELOVE.

If I were married, I would as soon part from my estate
as my wife.

LORD FOPPINGTON.

Now I would not, sunburn me if I would.   140

LORD MORELOVE.

Death! my lord, but since you are thus indifferent, why
would you needs marry a woman of so much merit? Could
not you have laid out your spleen upon some ill-natured
shrew that wanted the plague of an ill husband, and have
let her alone to some plain, honest man of quality that 145
would have deserved her?

LORD FOPPINGTON.

Why, faith, my lord, that might have been considered,
but I really grew so passionately fond of her fortune that,
curse catch me, I was quite blind to the rest of her good
qualities. For to tell you the truth, if it were possible the old 150
putt of a peer could have tossed her into t'other five
thousand pound for 'em, by my consent she should have
relinquished her merit and virtues to any of her younger
sisters.

SIR CHARLES EASY.

Ay, ay, my lord, virtues in a wife are good for nothing but 155
to make her proud and put the world in mind of her husband's faults.

LORD FOPPINGTON.

Right, Charles, and strike me blind, but the women of
virtue are grown such idiots in love, they expect of a man,
just as they do of a coach horse, that one's appetite, like 160
t'other's flesh, should increase by feeding.

SIR CHARLES EASY.

Right, my lord! and don't consider that *toujours chapons
bouillés* will never do with an English stomach.

141. my lord] *Q 1–2*; *om. P.*   150. were] *Q 1–2*; had been *P.*
141. indifferent, why] *Q 1–2*; in-   151–152. her . . . 'em] *Q 1–2*; one
different, my lord, why *P.*   in t'other five thousand for 'em *P.*
148. so] *P*; *om. Q 1–2.*

---

151. *putt*] blockhead.
162–163. *toujours chapons bouillés*] nothing but boiled capon; i.e., a tiresome diet.

LORD FOPPINGTON.

Ha, ha, ha! To tell you the truth, Charles, I have known
so much of that sort of eating that I now think, for an 165
hearty meal, no wildfowl in Europe is comparable to a joint
of Banstead mutton.

LORD MORELOVE.

How do you mean?

LORD FOPPINGTON.

Why, that for my part, I had rather have a plain slice of
my wife's woman than my guts full of e'er an ortolan 170
duchess in Christendom.

LORD MORELOVE.

But I thought, my lord, your business now at Windsor had
been your design upon a woman of quality.

LORD FOPPINGTON.

That's true, my lord, though I don't think your fine lady the
best dish myself, yet a man of quality can't be without such 175
things at his table.

LORD MORELOVE.

Oh! then you only desire the reputation of having an affair
with her?

LORD FOPPINGTON.

I think the reputation is the most inviting part of an amour
with most women of quality.   180

LORD MORELOVE.

Why so, my lord?

LORD FOPPINGTON.

Why, who the devil would run though all the degrees of
form and ceremony that lead one up to the last favor, if it
were not for the reputation of understanding the nearest
way to get over the difficulty?   185

LORD MORELOVE.

But, my lord, since the world sees you make so little of the
difficulty, does not the reputation of your being too general
an undertaker frighten the women from engaging with you?
For they say no man can love but one at a time.

172. your business] *Q 1–2*; your   186–187. since ... difficulty] *Q 1–2*;
chief business *P.*   *om. P.*
177. having] *Q 1–2*; *om. P.*   187. too] *Q 1–2*; so *P.*

---

167. *Banstead*] a small town near London.
170. *ortolan*] a small bird considered a delicacy.

–41–

LORD FOPPINGTON.

That's just one more than ever I came up to, for, stap my 190
breath, if ever I loved one in my life.

LORD MORELOVE.

How do you get 'em then?

LORD FOPPINGTON.

Why, sometimes as they get other people. I dress and let
them get me. Or, if that won't do, as I got my title, I buy
'em.   195

LORD MORELOVE.

But how can you, that profess indifference, think it worth
your while to come so often up to the price of a woman of
quality?

LORD FOPPINGTON.

Because you must know, my lord, that most of 'em begin now
to come down to reason; I mean, those that are to be had, 200
for some die fools. But with the wiser sort, 'tis not of late so
very expensive; now and then a *partie carrée*, a jaunt or two in
an hack to an Indian house, a little china, an odd thing for
a gown, or so, and in three days after you meet her at the
conveniency of trying it on *chez Mademoiselle D'Épingle*.   205

SIR CHARLES EASY.

Ay, ay, my lord, and when you are there, you know, what
between a little chat, a dish of tea, mademoiselle's good
humor and a *petite chanson* or two, the devil's in't if a man
can't fool away the time till he sees how it looks upon her by
candlelight. Ha, ha!   210

LORD FOPPINGTON.

Heh, heh! Well said, Charles. Igad, I fancy thee and I
have unlaced many a reputation there. Your great lady is as
soon undressed as her woman. Ha, ha!

LORD MORELOVE.

I could never find it so. The shame or scandal of a repulse
always made me afraid of attempting a woman of condition. 215

---

190. stap] *Q 1–2*; stop *P.*   205. on] *Q 1–2*; *om. P.*
194. them] *Q 1–2*; 'em *P.*   210. Ha, ha!] *Q 1–2*; *om. P.*
199. 'em] *Q 1–2*; them *P.*   213. Ha, ha!] *Q 1–2*; *om. P.*

202. *a partie carrée*] two couples.
203. *Indian house*] shop for Indian wares.

SIR CHARLES EASY.

Ha, ha! Igad, my lord, you deserve to be ill used. Your
modesty's enough to spoil any woman in the world; but my
lord and I understand the sex a little better. We see plainly
that women are only cold, as some men are brave, from the
modesty or fear of those that attack 'em.   220

LORD FOPPINGTON.

Right, Charles. A man should no more give up his heart to
a woman than his sword to a bully. They are both as insolent
as the devil after it.

SIR CHARLES EASY (*aside to* Lord Morelove).

How do you like that, my lord?

LORD MORELOVE.

Faith, I envy him. But, my lord, suppose your inclination 225
should stumble upon a woman truly virtuous, would not
a formal repulse from such a one put you strangely out
of countenance?

LORD FOPPINGTON.

Not at all, my lord, for if a man don't mind a box on the
ear in a fair struggle with a fresh country girl, why the 230
devil should he be concerned at an impertinent frown for
an attack upon a woman of quality?

LORD MORELOVE.

Then you have no notion of a lady's cruelty?

LORD FOPPINGTON.

Ha, ha, let me blood, if I think there's a greater jest in
nature. I am ready to crack my guts with laughing to see a 235
senseless flirt, because the creature happens to have a little
pride she calls virtue about her, give herself all the insolent
airs of resentment and disdain to an honest fellow that all the
while does not care three pinches of snuff if she and her
virtue were to run with their last favors through the first regi- 240
ment of guards. Ha, ha! It puts me in mind of an affair of
mine, so impertinent—

LORD MORELOVE.

Oh, that's impossible, my lord! Pray, let's hear it.

227. formal] *Q 1–2*; severe *P*.   231. devil] *Q 1–2*; deuce *P*.
229. on] *Q 1–2*; o' *P*.

LORD FOPPINGTON.

Why, I happened once to be well in a certain man of
quality's family, and his wife liked me.   245

LORD MORELOVE.

How do you know she liked you?

LORD FOPPINGTON.

Why, from the very moment I told her I liked her, she
never durst trust herself at the end of the room with me.

LORD MORELOVE.

That might be her not liking you.

LORD FOPPINGTON.

My lord, women of quality don't use to speak the thing 250
plain, but to satisfy you that I did not want encouragement,
I never came there in my life that she did not immediately
smile and borrow my snuffbox.

LORD MORELOVE.

She liked your snuff at least. Well, but how did she use
you?   255

LORD FOPPINGTON.

By all that's infamous, she jilted me.

LORD MORELOVE.

How? Jilt you?

LORD FOPPINGTON.

Ay, death's curse! She jilted me.

LORD MORELOVE.

Pray, let's hear.

LORD FOPPINGTON.

For when I was pretty well convinced she had a mind to 260
me, I one day made her a hint of an appointment, upon
which, with an insolent frown in her face (that made her look
as ugly as the devil) she told me that if ever I came thither
again her lord should know that she had forbidden me the
house before. Ha, ha! Did you ever hear of such a slut? 265

SIR CHARLES EASY.

Intolerable!

LORD MORELOVE.

But how did her answer agree with you?

---

244. be] *Q 1–2*; be very *P.*   252. that . . . not] *Q 1–2*; but she
248. the room] *Q 1–2*; a room *P.*   did *P.*
251. that] *Q 1–2*; *om. P.*   265. Ha, ha!] *Q 1–2*; *om. P.*

LORD FOPPINGTON.

Passionately well, for I stared full in her face and busted
out a-laughing, at which she turned upon her heel, gave a
crack with her fan like a coach whip, and bridled out of 270
the room with the air and complexion of an incensed turkey
cock.

LORD MORELOVE.

What did you do then?   *A Servant whispers* Sir Charles.

LORD FOPPINGTON.

I looked after her, gaped, threw up the sash, and fell a-
singing out of the window; so that you see, my lord, while 275
a man is not in love, there's no great affliction in missing
one's way to a woman.

SIR CHARLES EASY.

Ay, ay, you talk this very well, my lord. But now let's see
how you dare behave yourself upon action. Dinner's served
and the ladies stay for us. There's one within that has been 280
too hard for as brisk a man as yourself.

LORD MORELOVE.

I know whom you mean. Have a care, my lord. She'll prove
your courage for you.

LORD FOPPINGTON.

Will she! Then she's an undone creature. For let me tell
you, gentlemen, courage is the whole mystery of love, and of 285
more use than conduct is in war; for the bravest fellow in
Europe may beat his brains out against the stubborn walls
of a town, but—

Women, born to be controlled,
Stoop to the forward and the bold.   *Exeunt.* 290

268. Passionately] *Q 1–2*; Oh, passionately *P*.
268. busted] *Q 1–2*; burst *P*.
280. that] *Q 1–2*; *om. P*.

282. know whom] *Q 1–2*; guess who
P.
285. of love] *Q 1–2*; of making love
P.

ACT III

The scene continues.

Enter Lord Morelove *and* Sir Charles.

LORD MORELOVE.

So! Did not I bear up bravely?

SIR CHARLES EASY.

Admirably! With the best-bred insolence in nature! You insulted like a woman of quality when her country-bred husband's jealous of her in the wrong place.

LORD MORELOVE.

Ha, ha! Did you observe, when I first came into the room, 5 how carelessly she brushed her eyes over me, and when the company saluted me, stood all the while with her face to the window? Ha, ha!

SIR CHARLES EASY.

What astonished airs she gave herself when you asked her what made her so grave upon her old friends. 10

LORD MORELOVE.

And whenever I offered anything in talk, what affected care she took to direct her observations of it to a third person.

SIR CHARLES EASY.

I observed she did not eat above the rump of a pigeon all dinner time.

LORD MORELOVE.

And how she colored when I told her her ladyship had lost 15 her stomach.

SIR CHARLES EASY.

If you keep your temper she's undone.

LORD MORELOVE.

Provided she sticks to her pride, I believe I may.

SIR CHARLES EASY.

Ah, never fear her. I warrant in the humor she is in she would as soon part with her sense of feeling. 20

LORD MORELOVE.

Well, what's to be done next?

SIR CHARLES EASY.

Only observe her motions; for by her behavior at dinner, I am sure she designs to gall you with my Lord Foppington.

If so, you must even stand her fire, and then play my Lady
Graveairs upon her, whom I'll immediately pique and pre-   25
pare for your purpose.

LORD MORELOVE.

I understand you; the properest woman in the world, too,
for she'll certainly encourage the least offer from me in hopes
of revenging her late slights upon you.

SIR CHARLES EASY.

Right! And the very encouragement she gives you, at the   30
same time will give me a pretense to widen the breach
of my quarrel to her.

LORD MORELOVE.

Besides, Charles, I own I am fond of any attempt that
will forward a misunderstanding there, for your lady's sake.
A woman so truly good in her nature ought to have some-   35
thing more from a man than bare occasions to prove her
goodness.

SIR CHARLES EASY.

Why then, upon my honor, my lord, to give you a proof that
I am positively the best husband in the world, my wife—
never yet found me out.   40

LORD MORELOVE.

That may be her being the best wife in the world. She,
may be, won't find you out.

SIR CHARLES EASY.

Nay, if she won't tell a man of his faults when she sees 'em,
how the deuce should he mend 'em? But however, you see
I am going to leave 'em off as fast as I can.   45

LORD MORELOVE.

Being tired of a woman is indeed a pretty tolerable assurance of a man's not designing to fool on with her. —Here
she comes, and, if I don't mistake, brimful of reproaches.
You can't take her in better time. I'll leave you.

Enter Lady Graveairs.

LORD MORELOVE.

Your ladyship's most humble servant! Is the company   50
broke up, pray?

29. late] *Q 1–2*; *om. P.*   38. a] *Q 1–2*; *om. P.*

LADY GRAVEAIRS.

No, my lord, they were just talking of basset. My Lord
Foppington has a mind to tally, if your lordship would
encourage the table.

LORD MORELOVE.

O madam, with all my heart! But Sir Charles, I know, is   55
hard to be got to it; I'll leave your ladyship to prevail with
him.

Exit Lord Morelove.

Sir Charles *and* Lady Graveairs *salute coldly and trifle some time before
they speak.*

LADY GRAVEAIRS.

Sir Charles, I sent you a note this morning—

SIR CHARLES EASY.

Yes, madam, but there were some passages I did not expect
from your ladyship. You seemed to tax me with things that—   60

LADY GRAVEAIRS.

Look you, sir, 'tis not at all material whether I taxed you
with anything or no. I don't in the least desire to hear you
clear yourself; upon my word, you may be very easy as to
that matter; for my part I am mighty well satisfied that
things are as they are. All that I have to say to you is that   65
you need not give yourself the trouble to call at my lodgings
this afternoon, if you should have time, as you were pleased
to send me word—and so, your servant, sir—that's all.

Going.

SIR CHARLES EASY.

Hold, madam!

LADY GRAVEAIRS.

Look you, Sir Charles, 'tis not your calling me back that will   70
signify anything, I can assure you.

SIR CHARLES EASY.

Why this extraordinary haste, madam?

52. were] *Q 1–2*; are *P.*   66. not] *P*; *om. Q 1–2.*
64–65. satisfied that things] *Q 1–2*;
satisfied things *P.*

52. *basset*] a card game.
53. *tally*] deal.

LADY GRAVEAIRS.

In short, Sir Charles, I have taken a great many things
from you of late that you know I have often told you I
would positively bear no longer. But I see things are in vain   75
and the more people strive to oblige people, the less they are
thanked for't. And since there must be an end of one's ridi-
culousness one time or other, I don't see any time so proper
as the present, and therefore, sir, I desire you'd dispose
things accordingly. Your servant!   *Going, he holds her.*   80

SIR CHARLES EASY.

Nay, madam, let's start fair, however; you ought at
least to stay till I have got it in my head too, and then if we
must part—(*affectedly*)

    Adieu you silent grots and shady groves,
    Ye soft amusements of our growing loves;   85
    Adieu the whispered sighs that fanned the fire,
    And all the thrilling joys of young desire.

LADY GRAVEAIRS.

Oh, mighty well, sir! I am very glad we are at last come
to a right understanding, the only way I have long wished
for; not but I'd have you to know I see your design through   90
all this painted ease of resignation. I know you'd give your
eyes to make me uneasy now.

SIR CHARLES EASY.

Oh fie, madam! Upon my word, I would not make you uneasy if it were in my power.

LADY GRAVEAIRS.

O dear sir, you need not take such care, upon my word;   95
you'll find I can part with you without the least disorder.
I'll try, at least, and so once more, and forever, sir, your
servant. Not but you must give me leave to tell you, as my
last thought of you, too, that I do think—you are a villain.
                                   Exit hastily.

79–80. you'd . . . things] *Q 2*; you
would things *Q 1*; you would think
of things *P*.
80. S.D.] *P*; *om. Q 1–2*.
82. I . . . too] *Q 1–2*; I am as ready
as your ladyship *P*.

84. you] *Q 1–2*; ye *P*.
86. the whispered] *Q 1–2*; ye whispered *P*.
91. this] *Q 1–2*; your *P*.
92. eyes] *Q 1–2*; soul *P*.

SIR CHARLES EASY (*bowing low*).

> Oh, your very humble servant, madam. What a charming 100
> quality is a woman's pride, that's strong enough to refuse a
> man her favors—when he's weary of 'em. —Ah!

Lady Graveairs returns.

LADY GRAVEAIRS.

> Look you, Sir Charles, don't presume upon the easiness
> of my temper. For to convince you that I am positively in
> earnest in this matter, I desire you would let me have letters 105
> you have had of mine since you came to Windsor, and I
> expect you'll return the rest, as I will yours, as soon as we
> come to London.

SIR CHARLES EASY.

> Upon my faith, madam, I never keep any. I always put
> snuff in 'em, and so they wear out.   110

LADY GRAVEAIRS.

> Sir Charles, I must have 'em; for positively I won't stir
> without 'em.

SIR CHARLES EASY (*aside*).

> Ha! Then I must be civil, I see. —Perhaps, madam, I have
> no mind to part with them or you.

LADY GRAVEAIRS.

> Look you, sir, all those sort of things are in vain, now there's 115
> an end of everything between us. If you say you won't give
> 'em, I must even get 'em as well as I can.

SIR CHARLES EASY (*aside*).

> Ha! That won't do then, I find.

LADY GRAVEAIRS.

> Who's there? Mrs. Edging? Your keeping a letter, sir,
> won't keep me, I'll assure you.   120

Enter Edging.

EDGING.

> Did your ladyship call me, madam?

LADY GRAVEAIRS.

> Ay, child, pray do me the favor to fetch my hood and scarf
> out of the dining room.

113. S.D. (*aside*)] P; *om.* Q 1–2.   122. hood and] Q 1–2; *om.* P.
118. S.D. (*aside*)] P; *om.* Q 1–2.

EDGING.

Yes, madam.

SIR CHARLES EASY (*aside*).

Oh! Then there's hope again.   125

EDGING (*aside*).

Ha! She looks as if my master had quarreled with her. I
hope she's going away in a huff. She shan't stay for her
scarf, I warrant her. —This is pure.   *Exit.*

After some pause Lady Graveairs *speaks.*

LADY GRAVEAIRS.

Pray, Sir Charles, before I go give me leave now, after all,
to ask why you have used me thus?   130

SIR CHARLES EASY.

What is it you call usage, madam?

LADY GRAVEAIRS.

Why then, since you will have it, how comes it you have been
so grossly careless and neglectful of me of late? Only tell me
seriously wherein I have deserved it?

SIR CHARLES EASY.

Why then, seriously, madam—   135

Re-enter Edging *with a scarf.*

We are interrupted.

EDGING.

Here's your ladyship's scarf, madam.

LADY GRAVEAIRS.

Thank you, Mrs. Edging. Oh law! Pray, will you let somebody get me a chair to the door?

EDGING [*aside*].

Humph! She might have told me that at first, if she had   140
been in such haste to go.   *Exit.*

LADY GRAVEAIRS.

Now, sir.

125. S.D. (*aside*)] P; *om. Q 1–2.*   131. is it] *Q 1–2;* is't P.
128. S.D. *Exit*] *Q 1–2; Exit smiling*   134. it] *Q 1–2;* this P.
P.   135.1. *with a scarf*] P; *om. Q 1–2.*
128.1.] *Q 1–2; om. P.*   140. at first] *Q 1–2;* before P.

128. *pure*] excellent.

SIR CHARLES EASY.

Why then, seriously, I say, I am of late grown so very lazy
in my pleasures that I had rather lose a woman than go
through the plague and trouble of having or keeping her;   145
and to be free, I have found so much even in my acquaintance with you, whom I confess to be a mistress in the art
of pleasing, that I am from henceforth resolved to follow no
diversion that rises above the degree of an amusement;
and that woman that expects I should make her my business,   150
why, like my business, is then in a fair way of being forgot.
When once she comes to reproach me with vows, usage, and
stuff, I had as lief hear her talk of bills, bonds, and eject-
ments; her passion becomes as troublesome as a lawsuit,
and I would as soon converse with my solicitor. In short, I   155
shall never care sixpence for any woman that won't be
obedient.

LADY GRAVEAIRS.

I'll swear, sir, you have a very free way of treating people.
I am glad I am so well acquainted with your principles,
however. And you'd have me obedient?   160

SIR CHARLES EASY.

Why not? My wife's so, and I think she has as much
pretense to be proud as your ladyship.

LADY GRAVEAIRS.

Lard! Is there no chair to be had, I wonder?

Enter Edging.

EDGING.

Here's a chair, madam.

LADY GRAVEAIRS.

'Tis very well, Mrs. Edging. Pray will you let somebody   165
get me a glass of fair water?

EDGING (*aside*).

Ha! Her huff's almost over, I suppose. I see he's a villain
still.   *Exit.*

143. Why] *Q 1–2; om. P.*   167. Ha!] *Q 1–2;* Humh! *P.*
149. diversion] *Q 1–2;* pleasure *P.*   167. he's] *Q 1–2;* he is *P.*
149. an] *Q 1–2; om. P.*

166. *fair*] pure.

LADY GRAVEAIRS.

Well, that was the prettiest fancy about obedience, sure,
that ever was! Certainly a woman of condition must be 170
infinitely happy under the domination of so generous a
lover! But how came you to forget kicking and whipping
all this while? Methinks you should not have left so
fashionable an article out of your scheme of government.

SIR CHARLES EASY.

Um! No, there's too much trouble in that, though I have 175
known 'em of admirable use in the reformation of some
humorsome gentlewomen.

LADY GRAVEAIRS.

But one thing more and I have done. Pray, what degree
of spirit must the lady have that is to make herself happy
under so much freedom, order, and tranquillity?   180

SIR CHARLES EASY.

Oh, she must at least have as much spirit as your ladyship,
or she'd give me no pleasure in breaking it.

LADY GRAVEAIRS.

Oh, that would be troublesome. No, you had better take
one that's broken to your hand. There are such souls to be
hired, I believe; things that will rub your temples in an 185
evening till you fall fast asleep in their laps, creatures, too,
that think their wages a reward; I fancy, at last, that will
be the best method for the lazy passion of a married man
that has outlived his any other sense of gratification.

SIR CHARLES EASY.

Look you, madam, I have told you that reproaches will 190
never do your business with me. I have loved you very
well a great while; now you would have me love you better,
and longer, which is not my power to do, and I don't think
there's any plague upon earth like a dun that comes for
more money than one's ever likely to be able to pay.   195

LADY GRAVEAIRS.

A dun! Do you take me for a dun, sir! Do I come a-
dunning to you!   *Walks in an heat.*

181. Oh] *Q 1–2*; No *P*.   190–191. told . . . have] *Q 1–2*; *om.*
182. no] *Q 1–2*; *om. P*.   *P*.

SIR CHARLES EASY.

H'st! Don't expose yourself. Here's company.

LADY GRAVEAIRS.

I care not—a dun! You shall see, sir, I can revenge an
affront, though I despise the wretch that offers it. A dun! 200
Oh! I could die laughing at the fancy.   *Exit.*

SIR CHARLES EASY.

So! She's in admirable order. Here comes my lord, and I'm
afraid in the very nick of his occasion for her.

Enter Lord Morelove.

LORD MORELOVE.

Oh, Charles! Undone again! All's lost and ruined!

SIR CHARLES EASY.

What's the matter now?   205

LORD MORELOVE.

I have been playing the fool yonder even to contempt; my
senseless jealousy has confessed a weakness I shall never
forgive myself. She has insulted on it to that degree, too—I
can't bear the thought—O Charles! This devil still is
mistress of my heart, and I could dash my brains to think 210
how grossly too I've let her know it.

SIR CHARLES EASY.

Ah! How it would tickle her if she saw you in this condition. Ha, ha, ha!

LORD MORELOVE.

Prithee don't torture me. Think of some remedy for
present ease, or I shall burst.   215

SIR CHARLES EASY.

Well, well, let's hear, pray. What has she done to you?

LORD MORELOVE.

Why, ever since I left you she has treated me with so much
coolness and ill humor, and that thing of a lord with so
much laughing ease, such an acquainted, such a spiteful
familiarity, that she at last saw and triumphed in my 220
uneasiness.

198. H'st] *Q 2, P*; S't *Q 1*.   217. has] *Q 1–2*; *om. P*.
211. I've] *Q 1*; I have *Q 2, P*.   218. humor] *Q 1–2*; nature *P*.
214. remedy for] *Q 1–2*; *om. P*.   220. she at last] *Q 1–2*; at the last
216. you?] *Q 1–2*; you? Ha! ha! *P*.   she *P*.

SIR CHARLES EASY.

Well! and so you left the room in a pet?

LORD MORELOVE.

Oh, worse, worse still! For at last, with half shame and anger in my looks, I thrust myself before my lord, pressed her by the hand, and, in a whisper, trembling, begged her, 225 in pity of herself and me, to show her good humor only where she knew it was truly valued; at which she broke from me with a cold stare, sat her down by the peer, whispered him, and burst into a loud laughter in my face.

SIR CHARLES EASY.

Ha, ha! Then would I have given fifty pound to have seen 230 your face. Why, what in the name of common sense had you to do with humility? Will you never have enough on't? Death! 'twas setting a lighted match to gunpowder to blow yourself up.

LORD MORELOVE.

I see my folly now, Charles, but what shall I do with the 235 remains of life that she has left me?

SIR CHARLES EASY (*in a whining tone*).

Oh, throw it at her feet by all means, put on your tragedy face, catch fast hold of her petticoat, whip out your hand- kerchief, and in point blank verse desire her, one way or other, to make an end of the business. 240

LORD MORELOVE.

What a fool dost thou make me? *Smiling.*

SIR CHARLES EASY.

I only show you as you come out of her hands, my lord.

LORD MORELOVE.

How contemptibly have I behaved myself!

SIR CHARLES EASY.

That's according as you bear her behavior.

LORD MORELOVE.

Bear it? No! I thank thee, Charles, thou hast waked me 245 now, and if I bear it—! What have you done with my Lady Graveairs?

222. pet?] *Q 1–2*; pet? Ha! *P.*
224. before my lord] *Q 1–2*; be- tween my lord and her *P.*
236. remains] *Q 1–2*; small remains *P.*

236. S.D. (*in a whining tone*)] *P*; om. *Q 1–2.*
238–239. handkerchief] *Q 2*, *P*; handkercher *Q 1.*
241. S.D.] *Q 1–2*; om. *P.*

SIR CHARLES EASY.

Your business, I believe. She's ready for you. She's just gone downstairs, and if you don't make haste after her, I expect her back again with a knife or pistol, presently.   250

LORD MORELOVE.

I'll go this minute.

SIR CHARLES EASY.

No, stay a little, here comes my lord. We'll see what we can get out of him first.

LORD MORELOVE.

Methinks I now could laugh at her.

Enter Lord Foppington.

LORD FOPPINGTON.

Nay, prithee, Sir Charles, let's have a little of thee. We 255 have been so *chagrin* without thee that, stap my breath, the ladies are gone half asleep to church for want of thy company.

SIR CHARLES EASY.

That's hard indeed, while your lordship was among 'em. Is Lady Betty gone too?   260

LORD FOPPINGTON.

She was just upon the wing, but I caught her by the snuff-box, and she pretends to stay to see if I'll give it her again or no.

LORD MORELOVE.

Death! 'Tis that I gave her, and the only present she ever would receive from me.— (*Aside to* Sir Charles Easy.) 265 Ask him how he came by it.

SIR CHARLES EASY.

Prithee don't be uneasy. —Did she give it you, my lord?

LORD FOPPINGTON.

Faith, Charles, I can't say she did or she did not, but we were playing the fool and I took it—*à la*—pshaw! I can't tell thee in French neither, but Horace touches it to a 270 nicety; 'twas *pignus direptum male pertinaci*.

262. her] *P; om. Q 1–2.*

---

256. *chagrin*] dull.
271. *pignus . . . pertinaci*] the pledge snatched from her arms or finger faintly resisting (Horace, *Odes*, I, ix, 23–24).

LORD MORELOVE [*aside*].

So! but I must bear it. —If your lordship has a mind to the box, I'll stand by you in the keeping of it.

LORD FOPPINGTON.

My lord, I am passionately obliged to you, but I am afraid I can't answer your hazarding so much of the lady's 275 favor.

LORD MORELOVE.

Not at all, my lord. 'Tis possible I may not have the same regard to her frown that your lordship has.

LORD FOPPINGTON (*aside*).

That's a bite, I'm sure. I know he'd give a joint of his little finger to be as well with her as I am. —But here she comes! 280 Charles, stand by me. Must not a man be a vain coxcomb, now, to think this creature followed one?

SIR CHARLES EASY.

Oh! Nothing so plain, my lord.

LORD FOPPINGTON.

Flattering devil!

Enter Lady Betty.

LADY BETTY MODISH.

Pshaw! My Lord Foppington! Prithee don't play the fool 285 now, but give me my snuffbox. Sir Charles, help me to take it from him.   *Goes to* Lord Foppington.

SIR CHARLES EASY.

You know I hate trouble, madam.

LADY BETTY MODISH.

Pooh! You'll make me stay till prayers are half over now.

LORD FOPPINGTON.

If you'll promise me not to go to church I'll give it you.   290

LADY BETTY MODISH.

I'll promise nothing at all, for positively I will have it.

Struggles with him.

LORD FOPPINGTON.

Then comparatively I won't part with it.

Struggling with her.

---

279. That's a bite] *P*; That's bite   283. Oh!] *Q 1–2*; *om. P.*
Q 1–2.   287. S.D.] *Q 1–2*; *om. P.*
279. I know] *Q 1–2*; *om. P.*   292. it] *Q 1–2*; it. Ha! ha! *P.*

LADY BETTY MODISH.

> Oh, you devil! You have killed my arm! Oh! Well, seriously, if you'll let me have it, I'll give you a better.

LORD MORELOVE (*aside* to Sir Charles).

> O Charles! That has a view of distant kindness in it.   295

LORD FOPPINGTON.

> Nay, now I keep it superlatively; I find there's a secret value in it.

LADY BETTY MODISH.

> Oh, dismal! Upon my word, I am only ashamed to give it you. Do you think I would offer such an odious-fancied thing to anybody I had the least value for?   300

SIR CHARLES EASY (*aside to* Lord Morelove).

> Now it comes a little nearer, methinks it does not seem to be any kindness at all.

LORD FOPPINGTON.

> Why, really, madam, upon second view it has not extremely the mode of a lady's utensil; are you sure it never held anything but snuff?   305

LADY BETTY MODISH.

> Oh! You monster!

LORD FOPPINGTON.

> Nay, I only ask because it seems to me to have very much the air and fancy of Monsieur Smoakandsot's tobacco box.

LORD MORELOVE.

> I can bear no more.

SIR CHARLES EASY.

> Why don't, then. I'll step into the company and return to 310 your relief when there's occasion.   *Exit* Sir Charles.

LORD MORELOVE (*to* Lady Betty).

> Come, madam, will your ladyship give me leave to end the difference? Since the slightness of the thing may let you bestow it without any mark of favor, shall I beg it of your ladyship?   315

LADY BETTY MODISH.

> Oh, my lord, nobody sooner!—I beg you give it my lord.

---

293. seriously] *Q 1–2; om. P.*
311. when there's occasion] *Q 1–2;*
immediately *P.*

Looking very earnestly upon Lord Foppington, *who smiling gives it to* Lord Morelove *and then bows gravely to her.*

LORD MORELOVE.

Only to have the honor of restoring it to your lordship, and if there be any other trifle of mine your lordship has a fancy to, though it were a mistress, I don't know any person in the world that has so good a claim to my 320 resignation.

LORD FOPPINGTON.

O my lord, this generosity will distract me.

LORD MORELOVE.

My lord, I do you but common justice; but from your conversation, I had never known the true value of the sex. You positively understand 'em the best of any man 325 breathing, and therefore I think everyone of common prudence ought to resign to you.

LORD FOPPINGTON.

Then positively your lordship's the most obliging person in the world, for I'm sure your judgment can never like any woman that is not the finest creature in the universe. 330

Bowing to Lady Betty.

LORD MORELOVE.

Oh! Your lordship does me too much honor. I have the worst judgment in the world. No man has been more deceived in it.

LORD FOPPINGTON.

Then your lordship, I presume, has been apt to choose in a mask, or by candlelight. 335

LORD MORELOVE.

In a mask indeed, my lord, and of all masks the most dangerous.

LORD FOPPINGTON.

Pray what's that, my lord?

LORD MORELOVE.

A bare face.

LORD FOPPINGTON.

Your lordship will pardon me if I don't so readily compre- 340 hend how a woman's bare face can hide her face.

316.1. *very earnestly upon*] *Q 1–2*;   326. and] *Q 1–2*; *om. P.*
earnestly on P.

LORD MORELOVE.

It often hides her heart, my lord, and therefore I think
it a more dangerous mask than a piece of velvet. That's
rather a mark than a disguise of an ill woman. But
the mischiefs skulking behind a beauteous form give no 345
warning. They are always sure, fatal, and innumerable.

LADY BETTY MODISH.

Oh, barbarous aspersion! My Lord Foppington, have you
nothing to say for the poor women?

LORD FOPPINGTON.

I must confess, madam, nothing of this nature ever happened
in my course of amours. I always judge the beauteous 350
form of a woman to be the most agreeable part of her composition, and when a lady once does me the honor to toss
that into my arms, I think myself obliged in honor not to
quarrel about the rest of her equipage.

LADY BETTY MODISH.

Why, ay, my lord, there's some good humor in that, now.   355

LORD MORELOVE.

He's happy in a plain English stomach, madam. I could
recommend a dish that's perfectly to your lordships' *goût*,
where beauty is the only sauce to it.

LADY BETTY MODISH (*aside*).

So!

LORD FOPPINGTON.

My lord, when my wine's right, I never care it should be 360
zested. A fine woman, like a fine oyster, needs no sauce but
her own.

LORD MORELOVE.

I know some ladies would thank you for that opinion.

LADY BETTY MODISH.

My Lord Morelove's really grown such a churl to the
women, I don't only think he is not, but can't conceive how 365
he ever could be in love.

LORD MORELOVE.

Upon my word, madam, I once thought I was.   *Smiling.*

343. it a] *Q 1–2*; it sometimes a *P.*   353. honor] *Q 1–2*; good nature *P.*
352. a lady once] *Q 1–2*; once a   359. S.D. (*aside*)] *Q 1–2*; *om. P.*
lady *P.*   361–362. A . . . own.] *Q 1–2*; *om. P.*

361. *zested*] carbonated.

LADY BETTY MODISH.

Fie! fie! How could you think so? I fancy now you had
only a mind to domineer over some poor creature, and so
you thought you were in love, ha, ha!   370

LORD MORELOVE.

The lady I loved, madam, grew so unfortunate in her conduct that she at last brought me to treat her with the same
indifference and civility as I now pay your ladyship.

LADY BETTY MODISH.

And ten to one, just at that time she never thought you
such tolerable company, ha, ha!   375

LORD MORELOVE (*mimicking her manner*).

That I can't say, madam, for at that time she grew so
affected, there was no judging of her thoughts at all.

LADY BETTY MODISH.

What! And so you left the poor lady? Oh, you inconstant
creature!

LORD MORELOVE.

No, madam, to have loved her on had been inconstancy, 380
for she was never two hours together the same woman.

Lady Betty *and* Lord Morelove *seem to talk.*

LORD FOPPINGTON (*aside*).

Ha, ha, ha! He has a mind to abuse her, I find; so I'll ev'n
give him an opportunity of doing his business with her at
once forever. —My lord, I perceive your lordship's going
to be good company to the lady, and for her sake, I don't 385
think it good manners in me to disturb it.

Enter Sir Charles.

SIR CHARLES EASY.

My Lord Foppington—

LORD FOPPINGTON.

O Charles! I was just wanting thee. Hark thee! I have
three thousand secrets for thee. I have made such discoveries.
To tell thee all in one word—Morelove's as jealous of me 390
as the devil, heh, heh, ha!

375. ha, ha!] *Q 1–2*; *om. P.*   382. ev'n] *Q 1–2*; e'en *P.*
376. S.D. *manner] Q 1–2*; *om. P.*   386. disturb it] *Q 1–2*; disturb you
382. ha! He] *Q 1–2*; ha! I see he *P.*   *P.*

SIR CHARLES EASY.

    Is't possible? Has she given him any occasion?

LORD FOPPINGTON.

    Only rallied him to death upon my account. She told me
within, just now, she'd use him like a dog, and begged me
to draw off for an opportunity.   395

SIR CHARLES EASY.

    Oh! Keep in while the scent lies, and she's your own, my
lord.

LORD FOPPINGTON.

    I can't tell that, Charles, but I'm sure she's fairly unhar-
bored, and when once I throw off my inclinations, I usually
follow 'em till the game has enough on't, and between thee 400
and I she's pretty well blown, too. She can't stand long, I
believe, for curse catch me if I have not rid down half a
thousand pound after her already.

SIR CHARLES EASY.

    What do you mean?

LORD FOPPINGTON.

    I have lost five hundred to her at piquet since dinner.   405

SIR CHARLES EASY.

    You are a fortunate man, faith. You are resolved not to be
thrown out, I see.

LORD FOPPINGTON.

    Hang it! What should a man come out for, if he does not
keep up to the sport?

SIR CHARLES EASY.

    Well pushed, my lord.   410

LORD FOPPINGTON.

    Tayo! Have at her!

SIR CHARLES EASY.

    Down, down, my lord! Ah!—'ware hanches!

399. once I] *Q 1–2*; I once *P*.

---

396. *Keep . . . lies*] pursue the scent, as in the hunt.
398–399. *unharbored*] driven from cover.
401. *blown*] out of breath.
407. *thrown out*] thrown off the scent.
410. *pushed*] urged.
411. *Tayo!*] Tallyho!
412. *'ware hanches*] beware of bites.

LORD FOPPINGTON.

Ah, Charles! (*Embracing him.*) Prithee let's observe a
little. There's a foolish cur, now I have run her to a stand,
has a mind to be at her by himself, and thou shalt see 415
she won't stir out of her way for him. *They stand aside.*

LORD MORELOVE.

Ha, ha! Your ladyship's very grave of a sudden. You look
as if your lover had insolently recovered his common senses.

LADY BETTY MODISH.

And your lordship is so very gay, and unlike yourself, one
would swear you were just come from the pleasure of making 420
your mistress afraid of you.

LORD MORELOVE.

No, faith, quite contrary. For do you know, madam, I
have just found out that upon your account I have made
myself one of the most ridiculous puppies upon the face
of the earth? I have, upon my faith! Nay, and so extrav- 425
agantly such—ha, ha, ha!—that it's at last become a jest
even to myself, and I can't help laughing for the soul of me.

LADY BETTY MODISH (*disdainfully and aside*).

I want to cure him of that laugh now. —My lord, since
you are so generous, I'll tell you another secret. Do you
know, too, that I still find (spite of all your great wisdom 430
and my contemptible qualities, as you are pleased now and
then to call 'em)—do you know, I say, that I see under all
this, you still love me with the same helpless passion, and can
your vast foresight imagine that I won't use you accordingly
for these extraordinary airs you are pleased to give yourself? 435

LORD MORELOVE.

Oh, by all means, madam! 'Tis fit you should, and I expect
it, whenever it is in your power.— (*Aside.*) Confusion!

LADY BETTY MODISH.

My lord, you have talked to me this half hour without con-
fessing pain. (*Pauses and affects to gape.*) Only remember it.

LORD MORELOVE.

Hell and tortures! 440

413. Ah] *Q 1–2*; Ay *P.*
427. me.] *Q 1–2*; me. Ha! ha! ha!
P.

428. S.D. (*disdainfully and*] *Q 1–2*;
om. P.
434. that] *Q 1–2*; *om. P.*

LADY BETTY MODISH.

What did you say, my lord?

LORD MORELOVE.

Fire and furies!

LADY BETTY MODISH [*aside*].

Ha, ha! He's disordered. Now I am easy. —My Lord Foppington, have you a mind to your revenge at piquet?

LORD FOPPINGTON.

I have always a mind to an opportunity of entertaining 445 your ladyship, madam.

Lady Betty *coquets with* Lord Foppington.

LORD MORELOVE.

Charles, the insolence of this woman might furnish out a thousand devils.

SIR CHARLES EASY.

And your temper is enough to furnish out a thousand such women. Come away, I have business for you upon the 450 terrace.

LORD MORELOVE.

Let me but speak one word to her.

SIR CHARLES EASY.

Not a syllable. The tongue's a weapon you'll always have the worst at, for I see you have no guard, and she carries a devilish edge.   455

LADY BETTY MODISH.

My lord, don't let anything I've said frighten you away, for if you have the least inclination to stay and rail, you know the old conditions. 'Tis but your asking me pardon next day, and you may give your passion any liberty you think fit.   460

LORD MORELOVE.

Daggers and death!

SIR CHARLES EASY.

Are you mad?

LORD MORELOVE.

Let me speak to her now, or I shall burst.

446. S.D.] *P*; *om. Q 1–2.*   456. I've] *Q 1–2*; I have *P*.
447. Charles] *Q 1–2*; *om. P.*

SIR CHARLES EASY.

Upon condition you'll speak no more of her to me, my lord,
do as you please.   465

LORD MORELOVE.

Prithee pardon me! I know not what to do.

SIR CHARLES EASY.

Come along. I'll set you to work, I warrant you. Nay, nay,
none of your parting ogles! Will you go?

LORD MORELOVE.

Yes—and I hope for ever.

Exit Sir Charles *pulling away* Lord Morelove.

LORD FOPPINGTON.

Ha, ha, ha! Did ever mortal monster set up for a lover with   470
such unfortunate qualifications?

LADY BETTY MODISH.

Indeed, my Lord Morelove has something strangely singular
in his manner.

LORD FOPPINGTON.

I thought I should have burst to see the creature pretend to
raillery and give himself the airs of one of us. But run me   475
through, madam, your ladyship pushed like a fencing
master; that last thrust was a *coup de grâce*, I believe. I'm
afraid his honor will hardly meet your ladyship in haste
again.

LADY BETTY MODISH.

Not unless his second, Sir Charles, keeps him better in   480
practice, perhaps.— (*Aside*). Well, the humor of this
creature has done me signal service today. I must keep
it up for fear of a second engagement.

LORD FOPPINGTON.

Never was poor wit so foiled at his own weapon, sure.

LADY BETTY MODISH.

Wit! Had he ever any pretense to it?   485

LORD FOPPINGTON.

Ha, ha! He has not much in love, I think, though he wears
the reputation of a very pretty young fellow among some
sort of people. But strike me stupid, if ever I could discover

475. raillery] *Q 1–2*; rally *P.*   481. S.D. *Aside] P*; *om. Q 1–2.*
477. I'm] *Q 1–2*; I am *P.*

common sense in all the progress of his amours. He expects a woman should like him for endeavoring to convince her 490 that she has not one good quality belonging to the whole composition of her soul and body.

LADY BETTY MODISH.

That, I suppose, is only in a modest hope that she'll mend her faults to qualify herself for his vast merit, ha, ha!

LORD FOPPINGTON (*aside*).

Poor Morelove! I see she can't endure him. 495

LADY BETTY MODISH.

Or if one really had all those faults, he does not consider that sincerity in love is as much out of fashion as sweet snuff. Nobody takes it now.

LORD FOPPINGTON.

Oh, no mortal, madam, unless it be here and there a squire that's making his lawful court to the cherry-cheek charms of 500 my Lord Bishop's great fat daughter in the country.

LADY BETTY (*throwing her hand carelessly upon his*).

Oh, what a surfeiting couple has he put together!

LORD FOPPINGTON (*aside*).

Fond of me, by all that's tender! Poor fool, I'll give thee ease immediately. —But, madam, you were pleased just now to offer me my revenge at piquet. Now here's nobody within, 505 and I think we can't make use of a better opportunity.

LADY BETTY MODISH.

Oh, no! Not now, my lord! I have a favor I would fain beg of you first.

LORD FOPPINGTON.

But time, madam, is very precious in this place, and I shall not easily forgive myself if I don't take him by the 510 forelock.

LADY BETTY MODISH.

But I have a great mind to have a little more sport with my Lord Morelove first, and would fain beg your assistance.

LORD FOPPINGTON.

Oh, with all my heart!— (*Aside.*) And upon second thoughts, I don't know but piquing a rival in public may be 515 as good sport as being well with a mistress in private. For after

509. in] *P*; at *Q 1–2*.

all, the pleasure of a fine woman is like that of her own
virtue, not so much in the thing, as the reputation of having
it. —But how, madam, can I serve you in this affair?

LADY BETTY MODISH.

Why, methought as my Lord Morelove went out, he 520
showed a stern resentment in his look that seemed to
threaten me with rebellion and downright defiance. Now I
have a great fancy that you and I should follow him to the
terrace and laugh at his resolution before he has time to
put it in practice.   525

LORD FOPPINGTON.

And so punish his fault before he commits it! Ha, ha, ha!

LADY BETTY MODISH.

Nay, we won't give him time, if his courage should fail, to
repent it.

LORD FOPPINGTON.

Ha, ha! Let me blood, if I don't long to be at it! Ha, ha!

LADY BETTY MODISH.

Oh, 'twill be such diversion to see him bite his lips and 530
broil within, only with seeing us ready to split our sides in
laughing at nothing, ha, ha!

LORD FOPPINGTON (aside).

Ha, ha! I see the creature does really like me. —And then,
madam, to hear him hum a broken piece of a tune in
affectation of his not minding us—'twill be so foolish when 535
we know he loves us to death all the while, ha, ha!

LADY BETTY MODISH.

And if at last his sage mouth should open in surly contra-
diction of our humor, then will we, in pure opposition to his,
immediately fall foul upon everything that is not gallant and
fashionable. Constancy shall be the mark of age and ugliness, 540
virtue a jest; we'll rally discretion out of doors, lay gravity
at our feet, and only love, free love, disorder, liberty, and
pleasure be our standing principles.

LORD FOPPINGTON.

Madam, you transport me. For if ever I was obliged to
nature for any one tolerable qualification, 'twas positively 545

519. But how, madam] Q1–2;
Well, madam, just how P.

the talent of being exuberantly pleasant upon this subject.
I am impatient. My fancy's upon the wing already. Let's
fly to him.

LADY BETTY MODISH.

No. Stay till I am just got out. Our going together won't be
so proper.   550

LORD FOPPINGTON.

As your ladyship pleases, madam. But when this affair is
over, you won't forget that I have a certain revenge due.

LADY BETTY MODISH.

Ay! ay! After supper I am for you. Nay, you shan't stir a
step, my lord.

LORD FOPPINGTON (*seeing her to the door*).

Only to tell you, you have fixed me yours to the last exis- 555
tence of my soul's eternal entity.

LADY BETTY MODISH.

Oh, your servant!   *Exit* Lady Betty.

LORD FOPPINGTON.

Ha, ha! Stark mad for me, by all that's handsome! Poor
Morelove! That a fellow who has ever been abroad should
think a woman of her spirit is to be taken as the con-   560
federates do towns, by a regular siege, when so many of
the French successes might have shown him the surest way
is to whisper the governor. How can a coxcomb give himself
the fatigue of bombarding a woman's understanding, when
he may with so much ease make a friend of her constitu- 565
tion? I'll see if I can show him a little French play with
Lady Betty. Let me see—ay, I'll make an end of it the
old way—get her into piquet at her own lodgings, not
mind one tittle of my play, give her every game before
she's half up, that she may judge the strength of my inclina- 570
tion by my haste of losing up to her price; then of a sudden,
with a familiar leer, cry "Rat piquet!" sweep counters, cards
and money upon the floor, *et donc—l'affaire est faite.*   *Exit.*

547. No.] *Q 1–2*; No, no. *P.*   573. upon] *Q 1–2*; all upon *P.*

ACT IV

The scene, the terrace.
Enter Lady Easy *and* Lady Betty.

LADY EASY.

My dear, you really talk to me as if I were your lover,
and not your friend; or else I am so dull that by all you've
said I can't make the least guess at your real thoughts. Can
you be serious for a moment?

LADY BETTY MODISH.

Not easily, but I would do more to oblige you.   5

LADY EASY.

Then pray deal ingenuously, and tell me without reserve,
are you sure you don't love my Lord Morelove?

LADY BETTY MODISH.

Then seriously—I think not. But because I won't be
positive, you shall judge by the worst of my symptoms.
First, I own I like his conversation, his person has neither   10
fault nor beauty—well enough. I don't remember I ever
secretly wished myself married to him, or that I ever
seriously resolved against it.

LADY EASY.

Well! So far you are tolerably safe. But come, as to his
manner of addressing to you, what effect has that had?   15

LADY BETTY MODISH.

Humph! (*Smiling.*) I am not a little pleased to observe
few men follow a woman with the same fatigue and spirit
that he does me; am more pleased when he lets me use him
ill; and if ever I have a favorable thought of him, 'tis when
I see he can't bear that usage.   20

LADY EASY.

Have a care! that last is a dangerous symptom. He pleases
your pride, I find.

0.1. *the terrace*] *Q 1–2; the castle*
terrace P.
0.2. *Enter . . . Betty*] *Q 1–2; Enter*
Lady Betty *and* Lady Easy *P.*
6. ingenuously] *P*; ingeniously *Q 1–*
2.

15. addressing] *Q 1–2*; addressings
P.
16. Humph! (*Smiling.*)] *Q 1–2*; om.
P.

LADY BETTY MODISH.

    Oh, perfectly. In that I own no mortal ever can come up to
him.

LADY EASY

    But now, my dear, now comes the main point—jealousy.   25
Are you sure you have never been touched with it? Tell
me that with a safe conscience, and then I pronounce you
clear.

LADY BETTY MODISH.

    Nay, then I defy him, for positively I was never jealous in
my life.   30

LADY EASY.

    How, madam! Have you never been stirred enough to think
a woman strangely forward for being a little familiar in
talk with him? Or are you sure his gallantry to another
never gave you the least disorder?   Was you never, upon no
accident, in an apprehension of losing him?   35

LADY BETTY MODISH.

    Hah! Why, madam—bless me!—wh—wh—why sure, you
don't call this jealousy, my dear?

LADY EASY.

    Nay, nay, that is not the business. Have you ever felt
anything of this nature, madam?

LADY BETTY MODISH.

    Lord! Don't be so hasty, my dear—anything of this nature—   40
O lud! I swear I don't like it. Dear creature, bring me off
here. I am half frighted out of my wits.

LADY EASY.

    Nay, if you can rally upon't, your wound is not over-deep,
I'm afraid.

LADY BETTY MODISH.

    Well, that's comfortably said, however.   45

LADY EASY.

    But come, to the point! How far have you been jealous?

LADY BETTY MODISH.

    Why—oh, bless me!—he gave the music one night to my

34. Was] *Q 1–2*; were *P.*   42. I am] *Q 1–2*; for I am *P.*
36. Hah!] *Q 2, P*; Hay *Q 1.*

---

    47. *gave the music*] engaged an orchestra.

Lady Languish here upon the terrace, and though she and
I were very good friends, I remember I could not speak
to her in a week for't—oh!   50

LADY EASY.

Nay, now you may laugh if you can, for take my word,
the marks are upon you. But come, what else?

LADY BETTY MODISH.

Oh, nothing else, upon my word, my dear.

LADY EASY.

Well, one word more, and then I proceed to sentence.
Suppose you were heartily convinced that he actually   55
followed another woman?

LADY BETTY MODISH.

But, pray, my dear, what occasion is there to suppose any
such thing at all?

LADY EASY.

Guilty, upon my honor!

LADY BETTY MODISH.

Pshaw! I defy him to say that ever I owned any inclination   60
for him.

LADY EASY.

But you have given him terrible leave to guess it.

LADY BETTY MODISH.

If ever you see us meet again, you'll have but little reason
to think so, I can assure you.

LADY EASY.

That I shall see presently, for here comes Sir Charles, and   65
I am sure my lord can't be far off.

Enter Sir Charles.

SIR CHARLES EASY.

Servant, Lady Betty!—My dear, how do you do?

LADY EASY.

At your service, my dear! But pray, what have you done
with my Lord Morelove?

LADY BETTY MODISH.

Ay, Sir Charles, pray, how does your pupil do? Have you   70
any hopes of him? Is he docible?

54. proceed to] *Q 1–2*; give *P*.   62. But] *Q 1–2*; No, but *P*.

SIR CHARLES EASY.

Well, madam, to confess your triumph over me, as well as
him, I own my hopes of him are lost. I offered what I
could to his instruction, but he's incorrigibly yours, and
undone, and the news, I presume, does not displease your   75
ladyship.

LADY BETTY MODISH.

Fie, fie, Sir Charles, you disparage your friend. I am
afraid you don't take pains with him.

SIR CHARLES EASY.

Ha! I fancy, Lady Betty, your good nature won't let you
sleep a-nights. Don't you love dearly to hurt people?   80

LADY BETTY MODISH.

Oh, your servant! Then, without a jest, the man is so
unfortunate in his want of patience that let me die if I don't
often pity him.

SIR CHARLES EASY.

Strange goodness! Oh, that I were your lover for a month
or two.   85

LADY BETTY MODISH.

What then?

SIR CHARLES EASY.

I would make that pretty heart's blood of yours ache in a
fortnight.

LADY BETTY MODISH.

Ugh! I should hate you. Your assurance would make your
address intolerable.   90

SIR CHARLES EASY.

I believe it would, for I'd never address you at all.

LADY BETTY MODISH (*hitting him with her fan*).

Oh, you clown, you!

SIR CHARLES EASY.

Why, what to do? to feed a diseased pride, that's eternally
breaking out in the affectation of an ill nature that—in
my conscience I believe is but affectation?   95

LADY BETTY MODISH.

You, nor your friends have no great reason to complain of
my fondness, I believe. Ha, ha, ha!

84. Strange] *Q 1–2*; Ha! strange *P.*   96. friends] *Q 1–2*; friend *P.*
91. you] *P*; to you *Q 1–2*.

SIR CHARLES EASY (*looking earnestly on her*).
Thou insolent creature! How can you make a jest of a
man whose whole life's but one continued torment from
your want of common gratitude?　　　　　　　　100
LADY BETTY MODISH.
Torment! For my part, I really believe him as easy as you
are.
SIR CHARLES EASY.
Poor, intolerable affectation! You know the contrary,
you know him blindly yours, you know your power, and
the whole pleasure of your life's the poor and low abuse 105
of it.
LADY BETTY MODISH.
Pray, how do I abuse it?—if I have any power.
SIR CHARLES EASY.
You drive him to extremes that make him mad, then
punish him for acting against his reason. You've almost
turned his brain; his common judgment fails him; he's now, 110
at this very moment, driven by his despair upon a project,
in hopes to free him from your power, that I am sensible
(and so must anyone be that has his sense) of course must
ruin him with you forever. I almost blush to think of it,
yet your unreasonable disdain has forced him to it, and 115
should he now suspect I offered but a hint of it to you, as
in contempt of his design, I know he'd call my life to
answer it. But I have no regard to men in madness. I
rather choose for once to trust in your good nature, in hopes
the man whom your unwary beauty has made miserable, 120
your generosity would scorn to make ridiculous.
LADY BETTY MODISH.
Sir Charles, you charge me very home. I never had it in my
inclination to make anything ridiculous that did not deserve
it. Pray, what is this business you think so extravagant in
him?　　　　　　　　　　　　　　　　125
SIR CHARLES EASY.
Something so absurdly rash and bold you'll hardly forgive
ev'n me that tell it you.

119. choose] *P*; chose *Q 1–2*.

---

122. *charge . . . home*] accuse me directly.

-73-

LADY BETTY MODISH.

Oh fie! If it be a fault, Sir Charles, I shall consider it as
his, not yours. Pray, what is it?

LADY EASY.

I long to know, methinks.   130

SIR CHARLES EASY.

You may be sure he did not want my dissuasions from it.

LADY BETTY MODISH.

Let's hear it.

SIR CHARLES EASY.

Why, this man, whom I have known to love you with such
excess of generous desire, whom I have heard in his ecstatic
praises on your beauty talk till from the soft heat of his 135
distilling thoughts the tears have fallen—

LADY BETTY MODISH (*blushing*).

Oh, Sir Charles—

SIR CHARLES EASY.

Nay, grudge not, since 'tis past, to hear what was (though
you contemned it) once his merit. But now, I own, that
merit ought to be forgotten.   140

LADY BETTY MODISH.

Pray, sir, be plain.

SIR CHARLES EASY.

This man, I say, whose unhappy passion has so ill succeeded
with you, at last has forfeited all his hopes (into which,
pardon me, I confess my friendship had lately flattered him),
his hopes of ev'n deserving now your lowest pity or regard. 145

LADY BETTY MODISH.

You amaze me, for I can't suppose his utmost malice dares
assault my reputation. And what—

SIR CHARLES EASY.

No, but he maliciously presumes the world will do it for
him; and indeed, he has taken no unlikely means to make
'em busy with their tongues, for he is this minute upon the 150
open terrace in the highest public gallantry with my Lady
Graveairs. And to convince the world and me, he said, he
was not that tame lover we fancied him, he'd venture to give
her the music tonight. Nay, I heard him, before my face,

---

150. 'em] *Q 1–2*; them *P*.   150. minute] *Q 1–2*; moment *P*.

speak to one of the hautboys to engage the rest, and desired 155
they would all take their directions only from my Lady
Graveairs.

LADY BETTY MODISH.

My Lady Graveairs! Truly, I think my lord's very much in
the right on't. For my part, Sir Charles, I don't see anything in this that's so very ridiculous, nor indeed that 160
ought to make me think either the better or the worse of
him for't.

SIR CHARLES EASY.

Pshaw! Pshaw! Madam, you and I know 'tis not in his
power to renounce you. This is but the poor disguise of a
resenting passion vainly ruffled to a storm, which the least 165
gentle look from you can reconcile at will and laugh into
a calm again.

LADY BETTY MODISH.

Indeed, Sir Charles, I shan't give myself that trouble, I
believe.

SIR CHARLES EASY.

So I told him, madam. "Are not all your complaints," said 170
I, "already owing to her pride, and can you suppose this
public defiance of it (which you know you can't make
good too) won't incense her more against you?" "That's
what I'd have," said he, starting wildly. "I care not what
becomes of me, so I but live to see her piqued at it."   175

LADY BETTY MODISH (*disordered*).

Upon my word, I fancy my lord will find himself mistaken.
I shan't be piqued, I believe. I must first have a value for
the thing I lose, before it piques me. "Piqued!" Ha, ha, ha!

SIR CHARLES EASY.

Madam, you've said the very thing I urged to him. "I
know her temper so well," said I, "that though she doted 180
on you, if you once stood out against her, she'd sooner burst
than show the least distant motion of uneasiness."

LADY BETTY MODISH.

I can assure you, Sir Charles, my lord won't find himself
deceived in your opinion. "Piqued!"

161. the worse] *Q 1–2*; worse *P.*   182. distant] *Q 1–2*; *om. P.*

155. *hautboys*] oboes.

SIR CHARLES EASY (*aside*).

> She has it! 185

LADY EASY.

> Alas, poor woman! How little do our passions make us!

LADY BETTY MODISH.

> Not but I would advise him to have a little regard to my
> reputation in this business. I would have him take heed of
> publicly affronting me.

SIR CHARLES EASY.

> Right, madam, that's what I strictly warned him of; for 190
> among friends, whenever the world sees him follow another
> woman, the malicious tea-tables will be very apt to be free
> with your ladyship.

LADY BETTY MODISH.

> I'd have him consider that, methinks.

SIR CHARLES EASY.

> But alas, madam, 'tis not in his power to think with reason. 195
> His mad resentment has destroyed ev'n his principles of
> common honesty. He considered nothing but a senseless,
> proud revenge, which in this fit of lunacy 'tis impossible
> that either threats or dangers can dissuade him from.

LADY BETTY MODISH.

> What! Does he defy me, threaten me? Then he shall see that 200
> I have passions too, and know as well as he to stir my heart
> 'gainst any pride that dares insult me. Does he suppose I
> fear him? Fear the little malice of a slighted passion that my
> own scorn has stung to a despised resentment! Fear him!
> Oh! it provokes me to think he dares have such a thought. 205

LADY EASY.

> Dear creature, don't disorder yourself so.

LADY BETTY MODISH (*walking disordered*).

> Let me but live to see him once more within my power,
> and I'll forgive the rest of fortune.

LADY EASY (*aside*).

> Well! Certainly I am very ill-natured, for though I see this
> news has disturbed my friend, I can't help being pleased 210
> with any hopes of my Lady Graveairs being otherwise dis-

---

199. dangers] *Q 1–2*; danger *P.*   209. S.P. LADY EASY] *Q 1–2*; Lady
204. stung to] *Q 1–2*; stung into *P.*   Betty *P.*

posed of. —My dear, I am afraid you have provoked her a
little too far.

SIR CHARLES EASY.

Pshaw! Not at all. You shall see, I'll sweeten her, and she'll
cool like a dish of tea.   215

LADY BETTY MODISH.

I may see him with his complaining face again—

SIR CHARLES EASY.

I am sorry, madam, you so wrongly judge of what I've told
you. I was in hopes to have stirred your pity, not your anger.
I little thought your generosity would punish him for faults
which you yourself resolved he should commit. —Yonder 220
he comes, and all the world with him. Might I advise you,
madam, you should not resent this thing at all. I would not
so much as stay to see him in his fault; nay, I'd be the last
that heard of it. Nothing can sting him more, or so justly
punish his folly, as your utter neglect of it.   225

LADY EASY.

Come, dear creature, be persuaded and go home with me;
indeed, it will show more indifference to avoid him.

LADY BETTY MODISH.

No, madam, I'll oblige his vanity for once, and stay and let
him see how strangely he has piqued me.

SIR CHARLES EASY (aside).

Oh, not at all to speak of; you had as good part with a 230
little of that pride of yours, or I shall yet make it a very
troublesome companion to you.

                    Goes from them and whispers Lord Morelove.

Enter Lord Foppington, *and a little after*, Lord Morelove, Lady
Graveairs *and other ladies.*

LORD FOPPINGTON.

Ladies, your servant! Oh! We have wanted you beyond
reparation—such diversion!

LADY BETTY MODISH.

Well, my lord! Have you seen my Lord Morelove?   235

214. Pshaw!] *Q 1–2*; Oh! *P.*   227. indifference] *P*;   indifferent
227. indeed] *Q 1–2*; *om. P.*   *Q 1–2.*

LORD FOPPINGTON.

Seen him!—ha, ha, ha!—I have such things to tell you, madam, you'll die.

LADY BETTY MODISH.

Oh, pray let's have 'em, for I was never in a better humor to receive them.

LORD FOPPINGTON.

Hark you!   *They whisper.* 240

LORD MORELOVE (*to* Sir Charles).

So, she's engaged already.

SIR CHARLES EASY.

So much the better; make but a just advantage of my success, and she's undone.

LORD FOPPINGTON. LADY BETTY MODISH.

Ha, ha, ha!

SIR CHARLES EASY.

You see already what ridiculous pains she's taking to stir 245 your jealousy and cover her own.

LORD FOPPINGTON. LADY BETTY MODISH.

Ha, ha, ha!

LORD MORELOVE.

Oh, never fear me, for upon my word, it now appears ridiculous even to me.

SIR CHARLES EASY (*whispers* Lord Morelove).

And hark you—   250

LADY BETTY MODISH.

Ha, ha! and so the widow was as full of airs as his lordship?

SIR CHARLES EASY (*aside*).

Only observe that, and 'tis impossible you can fail.

LORD MORELOVE.

Dear Charles, you have convinced me, and I thank you.

LADY GRAVEAIRS.

My Lord Morelove! What! Do you leave us?

LORD MORELOVE.

Ten thousand pardons, madam. I was but just—   255

LADY GRAVEAIRS.

Nay, nay, no excuses, my lord, so you will but let us have you again.

236. I have] *Q 1–2*; O I have *P.*   251. Ha, ha!] *Q 1–2*; *om. P.*
238. have] *Q 1–2*; hear *P.*

SIR CHARLES EASY (*aside to* Lady Graveairs).

I see you have good humor, madam, when you like your
company.

LADY GRAVEAIRS.

And you, I see, for all your mighty thirst of dominion, 260
could stoop to be obedient, if one thought it worth one's
while to make you so. Ha, ha!

SIR CHARLES EASY (*aside*).

Ha! Power would make her an admirable tyrant.

LADY EASY (*aside, observing* Sir Charles *and* Lady Graveairs).

So! There's another couple have quarreled too, I see. Those
airs to my Lord Morelove look as if designed to recover Sir 265
Charles into jealousy. I'll endeavor to join the company
and, it may be, that will let me into the secret. —My Lord
Foppington, I vow this is very uncomplaisant, to engross so
agreeable a part of the company to yourself.

SIR CHARLES EASY.

Nay, my lord, that is not fair, indeed, to enter into secrets 270
among friends. Ladies, what say you? I think we ought to
declare against it.

LADIES.

Oh, no secrets, no secrets!

LADY BETTY MODISH.

Well, ladies, I ought only to ask your pardon. My lord's
excusable, for I would haul him into a corner. 275

LORD FOPPINGTON.

I swear it's very hard, ho! I observe two people of extreme
condition can no sooner grow particular but the multitude
of both sexes are immediately up, and think their pro-
perties invaded.

LADY BETTY MODISH.

Odious multitude! 280

LORD FOPPINGTON.

Perish the *canaille*!

LADY GRAVEAIRS.

Oh, my lord, we women have all reason to be jealous of
Lady Betty Modish's power.

262. Ha, ha!] *Q 1–2*; *om. P.*   281. the] *P*; that *Q 1–2*.
264. see] *Q 1–2*; find *P.*

281. *canaille*] rabble.

LORD MORELOVE (*to* Lady Betty).

As the men, madam, all have of my Lord Foppington;
beside, favorites of great merit discourage those of an 285
inferior class for their prince's service. He has already lost
you one of your retinue, madam.

LADY BETTY MODISH.

Not at all, my lord, he has only made room for another.
One must sometimes make vacancies, or there could be no
preferments.   290

LORD FOPPINGTON.

Ha, ha! Ladies' favors, my lord, like places at court, are
not always held for life, you know.

LADY BETTY MODISH.

No, indeed! If they were, the poor fine women would be
all used like their wives, and no more minded than the
business of the nation.   295

LADY EASY.

Have a care, madam. An undeserving favorite has been the
ruin of many a prince's empire.

LORD FOPPINGTON.

Upon my soul, Lady Betty, we must grow more discreet, for
positively, if we go on at this rate, we shall have the world
throw you under the scandal of constancy, and I shall have 300
all the swords of condition at my throat for a monopolist.

LORD MORELOVE.

Oh! There's no great fear of that, my lord; though the
men of sense give it over, there will be always some idle
fellows vain enough to believe their merit may succeed as
well as your lordship's.   305

LADY BETTY MODISH.

Or if they should not, my lord, cast lovers, you know, need
not fear being long out of employment while there are so
many well-disposed people in the world. There are generally neglected wives, stale maids, or charitable widows,
always ready to relieve the necessities of a disappointed 310
passion—and, by the way, hark you, Sir Charles!

290. preferments] *P*; preferment   298. Upon] *Q 1–2*; Ha! ha! upon
Q 1–2.   *P*.
                                        302. great] *P*; such *Q 1–2*.

LORD MORELOVE (*aside*).

So! She is stirred, I see, for all her pains to hide it. She would hardly have glanced an affront at a woman she was not piqued at.

LADY GRAVEAIRS (*aside*).

That wit was thrown at me, I suppose; but I'll return it.   315

LADY BETTY MODISH (*softly to* Sir Charles).

Pray, how came you all this while to trust your mistress so easily?

SIR CHARLES EASY.

One is not so apt, madam, to be alarmed at the liberties of an old acquaintance as perhaps your ladyship ought to be at the resentment of an hard-used, honorable lover.   320

LADY BETTY MODISH.

Suppose I were alarmed, how does that make you easy?

SIR CHARLES EASY.

Come, come, be wise at last; my trusting them together may easily convince you that (as I told you before) I know his addresses to her are only outward, and 'twill be your own fault now if you let him go on till the world thinks him in 325 earnest, and a thousand busy tongues are set upon malicious inquiries into your reputation.

LADY BETTY MODISH.

Why, Sir Charles, do you suppose while he behaves himself as he does that I won't convince him of my indifference?

SIR CHARLES EASY.

But hear me, madam.   330

LADY GRAVEAIRS (*aside*).

The air of that whisper looks as if the lady had a mind to be making her peace again, and 'tis possible his worship's being so busy in the matter too may proceed as much from his jealousy of my lord with me as friendship to her; at least I fancy so, therefore I'm resolved to keep her still 335 piqued and prevent it, though it be only to gall him. —Sir Charles, that is not fair, to take a privilege that you just now declared against in my Lord Foppington.

LORD MORELOVE.

Well observed, madam.

312. She is] *Q 1–2*; she's *P.*   337. that] *Q 1–2*; *om. P.*

LADY GRAVEAIRS.

Beside, it looks so affected to whisper when everybody 340
guesses the secret.

LORD MORELOVE.

Ha, ha, ha!

LADY BETTY MODISH.

Oh, madam, your pardon in particular! But 'tis possible
you may be mistaken. The secrets of people that have any
regard to their actions are not so soon guessed as theirs 345
that have made a confidant of the whole town.

LORD FOPPINGTON.

Ha, ha, ha!

LADY GRAVEAIRS.

A coquette, in her affected airs of disdain to a revolted
lover, I'm afraid must exceed your ladyship in prudence, not
to let the world see at the same time she'd give her eyes to 350
make her peace with him. Ha, ha!

LORD MORELOVE.

Ha, ha, ha!

LADY BETTY MODISH.

'Twould be a mortification indeed if it were in the power
of a fading widow's charms to prevent it; and the man
must be miserably reduced, sure, that could bear to live 355
buried in woolen, or take up with the motherly comforts
of a swan-skin petticoat. Ha, ha!

LORD FOPPINGTON.

Ha, ha, ha!

LADY GRAVEAIRS.

Widows, it seems, are not so squeamish to their interest.
They know their own minds and take the man they like, 360
though it happens to be one that a froward, vain girl has
disobliged and is pining to be friends with.

LORD MORELOVE.

Nay, though it happens to be one that confesses he once
was fond of a piece of folly and afterwards ashamed on't.

---

356. *buried in woolen*] As part of a program to promote the English wool
industry the dead were required to be buried in woolen. This could be
avoided by payment of a fine.

357. *swan-skin*] a kind of flannel.

LADY BETTY MODISH.

Nay, my lord, there's no standing against two of you.   365

LORD FOPPINGTON.

No, faith, that's odds at tennis, my lord. Not but, if your
ladyship pleases, I'll endeavor to keep your backhand a
little, though, upon my soul, you may safely set me up at the
line, for knock me down if ever I saw a rest of wit better
played than that last in my life. —What say you, madam, 370
shall we engage?

LADY BETTY MODISH.

As you please, my lord.

LORD FOPPINGTON.

Ha, ha, ha! *Allons! Tout de bon, jouez, mi lor.*

LORD MORELOVE.

Oh, pardon me, sir, I shall never think myself in anything
a match for the lady.   375

LORD FOPPINGTON.

To you, madam.

LADY BETTY MODISH.

That's much, my lord, when the world knows you have
been so many years teasing me to play the fool with you.

LORD FOPPINGTON.

Ah! *Bien joué!*

LORD MORELOVE.

At that game I confess your ladyship has chosen a much 380
properer person to improve your hand with.

LORD FOPPINGTON.

To me, madam. —My lord, I presume whoever the lady
thinks fit to play the fool with will at least be able to give
as much envy as the wise person that had not wit enough to
keep well with her when he was so.   385

LADY GRAVEAIRS.

Oh, my lord! Both parties must needs be greatly happy, for
I dare swear neither will have any rivals to disturb 'em.

LORD MORELOVE.

Ha, ha!

379. *joué!*] *Q 1–2; joué!* Ha! ha! ha! *P.*

_____

368–369. *set . . . line*] put me near the net.
369. *rest of wit*] a rally.

LADY BETTY MODISH.

None that will disturb 'em, I dare swear.

LORD FOPPINGTON.

Ha, ha, ha! 390

LORD MORELOVE. LADY GRAVEAIRS. LADY BETTY MODISH.

Ha, ha, ha!

SIR CHARLES EASY.

I don't know, gentlefolks—but you are all in extreme good humor, methinks. I hope there's none of it affected.

LADY EASY (*aside*).

I should be loath to answer for any but my Lord Foppington.

LADY BETTY MODISH.

Mine is not, I'll swear. 395

LORD MORELOVE.

Nor mine, I'm sure.

LADY GRAVEAIRS.

Mine's sincere, depend upon't.

LORD FOPPINGTON.

And may the eternal frowns of the whole sex doubly demme if mine is not.

LADY EASY.

Well, good people, I am mighty glad to hear it. You have all 400
performed extremely well, but if you please you shall ev'n give over your wit now, while it is well.

LADY BETTY MODISH (*to herself*).

Now I see his humor I'll stand it out, if I were sure to die for't.

SIR CHARLES EASY (*aside to* Lady Betty).

You should not have proceeded so far with my Lord 405
Foppington after what I had told you.

LADY BETTY MODISH.

Pray, Sir Charles, give me leave to understand myself a little.

SIR CHARLES EASY.

Your pardon, madam, I thought a right understanding would have been for both your interests and reputation. 410

395. S.P. LADY BETTY MODISH] *P*;
Lady Easy *Q 1–2*.

LADY BETTY MODISH.

For his, perhaps.

SIR CHARLES EASY.

Nay, then, madam, it's time for me to take care of my friend.

LADY BETTY MODISH.

I never in the least doubted your friendship to him in
anything that was to show yourself my enemy.

SIR CHARLES EASY.

Since I see, madam, you have so ungrateful a sense of 415
my Lord Morelove's merit and my service, I shall never be
ashamed of using my power henceforth to keep him
entirely out of your ladyship's.   *Goes from her.*

LADY BETTY MODISH (*to herself*).

Was ever anything so insolent! I could find in my heart to
run the hazard of a downright compliance if it were only 420
to convince him that my power, perhaps, is not inferior to
his.

LADY EASY.

My Lord Foppington, I think you generally lead the company upon these occasions. Pray, will you think of some
prettier sort of diversion for us than parties and whispers.   425

LORD FOPPINGTON.

What say you, ladies? Shall we step and see what's done at
the basset table?

LADY BETTY MODISH.

With all my heart, Lady Easy.

LADY EASY.

I think 'tis the best thing we can do, and because we
won't part tonight, you shall all sup where you dined. — 430
What say you, my lord?

LORD MORELOVE.

Your ladyship may be sure of me, madam.

LORD FOPPINGTON.

Ay! ay! We'll all come.

LADY EASY.

Then pray let's change parties a little. My Lord Foppington,
you shall squire me.   435

418. S.D.] *Q 1–2; om. P.*

LORD FOPPINGTON.

 Oh, you do me honor, madam.

LADY BETTY MODISH.

 My Lord Morelove, pray let me speak with you.

LORD MORELOVE.

 Me, madam?

LADY BETTY MODISH.

 If you please, my lord.

LORD MORELOVE (*aside*).

 Ha! That look shot through me! What can this mean? 440

LADY BETTY MODISH.

 This is no proper place to tell you what it is. But there is one thing I'd fain be truly answered in. I suppose you'll be at my Lady Easy's by and by, and if you'll give me leave there—

LORD MORELOVE.

 If you please to do me that honor, madam, I shall certainly be there. 445

LADY BETTY MODISH.

 That's all, my lord.

LORD MORELOVE.

 Is not your ladyship for walking?

LADY BETTY MODISH.

 If your lordship dare venture with me.

LORD MORELOVE (*taking her hand*).

 Oh, madam!— (*Aside.*) How my heart dances, what heavenly music's in her voice, when softened into kindness. 450

LADY BETTY MODISH [*aside*].

 Ha! His hand trembles; Sir Charles may be mistaken.

LORD FOPPINGTON.

 My Lady Graveairs, you won't let Sir Charles leave us?

LADY GRAVEAIRS.

 No, my lord, we'll follow you.— (*To* Sir Charles.) Stay a little.

SIR CHARLES EASY.

 I thought your ladyship designed to follow 'em. 455

LADY GRAVEAIRS.

 Perhaps I'd speak with you.

---

448. dare] *Q 1–2*; dares *P.*

SIR CHARLES EASY.

But, madam, consider we shall certainly be observed.

LADY GRAVEAIRS.

Lord, sir! If you think it such a favor—!   *Exit hastily.*

SIR CHARLES EASY.

Is she gone? Let her go, etc.   *Exit singing.*

---

459. *Is . . . etc.*] the opening lines of an anonymous song "The Careless Swain" in *Westminster Drollery*, Part I (1671).

ACT V

[V.i]   *The scene continues.*
                Enter Sir Charles *and* Lord Morelove.

SIR CHARLES EASY.

Come a little this way. My Lady Graveairs had an eye
upon me as I stole off, and I'm apprehensive will make
use of any opportunity to talk with me.

LORD MORELOVE.

Oh, we are pretty safe here. Well, you were speaking of
Lady Betty.   5

SIR CHARLES EASY.

Ay, my lord. I say, notwithstanding all this sudden change
of her behavior, I would not have you yet be too secure of
her, for between you and I, since, as I told you, I have
professed myself an open enemy to her power with you, 'tis
not impossible but this new air of good humor may very   10
much proceed from a little woman's pride of convincing me
you are not yet out of her power.

LORD MORELOVE.

Not unlikely. But still, can we make no advantage of it?

SIR CHARLES EASY.

That's what I have been thinking of. Look you—death! My
Lady Graveairs!   15

LORD MORELOVE.

Ha! She will have audience, I find.

SIR CHARLES EASY.

There's no avoiding her. The truth is, I have owed her a
little good nature a great while. I see there is but one way of
getting rid of her; I must ev'n appoint her a day of payment
at last. If you'll step into my lodgings, my lord, I'll just give   20
her an answer and be with you in a moment.

                                        Exit Lord Morelove.

            Enter Lady Graveairs *on the other side.*

LADY GRAVEAIRS.

Sir Charles!

SIR CHARLES EASY.

Come, come, no more of these reproachful looks! You'll
find, madam, I have deserved better of you than your

jealousy imagines. Is it a fault to be tender of your repu-   25
tation? Fie, fie! This may be a proper time to talk, and of
my contriving, too. You see I just now shook off my Lord
Morelove on purpose.

LADY GRAVEAIRS.
May I believe you?

SIR CHARLES EASY.
Still doubting my fidelity, and mistaking my discretion for   30
want of good nature.

LADY GRAVEAIRS.
Don't think me troublesome; for I confess 'tis death to
think of parting with you. Since the world sees, for you I
have neglected friends and reputation, have stood the little
insults of disdainful prudes that envied me, perhaps, your   35
friendship, have borne the freezing looks of near and
general acquaintance—since this is so, don't let 'em ridicule
me too and say my foolish vanity undid me; don't let 'em
point at me as a cast mistress.

SIR CHARLES EASY.
You wrong me to suppose the thought; you'll have better of   40
me when we meet. When shall you be at leisure?

LADY GRAVEAIRS.
I confess, I would see you once again. If what I have more
to say prove ineffectual, perhaps it might convince me then
'tis in my interest to part with you. Can you come tonight?

SIR CHARLES EASY.
You know we have company, and I'm afraid they'll stay too   45
late. Can't it be before supper? What's o'clock now?

LADY GRAVEAIRS.
It's almost six.

SIR CHARLES EASY.
At seven, then, be sure of me; till when, I'd have you go
back to the ladies to avoid suspicion, and about that
time—have the vapors.   50

LADY GRAVEAIRS.
May I depend upon you?   *Exit* Lady Graveairs.

SIR CHARLES EASY.
Depend on everything! A very troublesome business this.
Send me once fairly rid on't; if ever I'm caught in an
honorable affair again! A debt, now, that a little ready civility

and away would satisfy, a man might bear with, but to 55
have a rent charge upon one's good nature, with an un-
conscionable long scroll of arrears too, that would eat out
the profits of the best estate in Christendom—ah! intolerable! Well, I'll ev'n to my lord and shake off the thoughts
on't.

Exit. 60

Enter Lady Betty *and* Lady Easy.

LADY BETTY MODISH.

I observe, my dear, you have usually this great fortune
at play. It were enough to make one suspect your good luck
with an husband.

LADY EASY.

Truly, I don't complain of my fortune either way.

LADY BETTY MODISH.

Prithee tell me—you are often advising me to it— are 65
there those real, comfortable advantages in marriage that
our old aunts and grandmothers would persuade us of?

LADY EASY.

Upon my word, if I had the worst husband in the world,
I should still think so.

LADY BETTY MODISH.

Ay, but then the hazard of not having a good one, my dear. 70

LADY EASY.

You may have a good one, I dare say, if you don't give airs
till you spoil him.

LADY BETTY MODISH.

Can there be the same dear, full delight in giving ease
as pain? Oh, my dear! the thought of parting with one's
power is insupportable! 75

LADY EASY.

And the keeping it, till it dwindles into no power at all, is
most ruefully foolish.

LADY BETTY MODISH.

But still, to marry before one's heartily in love—

LADY EASY.

Is not half so formidable a calamity. But if I have any eyes,
my dear, you'll run no great hazard of that in venturing 80

70. of not] *P*; of *Q 1–2.*

upon my Lord Morelove. You don't know, perhaps, that within this half hour the tone of your voice is strangely softened to him, ha! ha! ha! ha!

LADY BETTY MODISH.

My dear, you are positively, one or other, the most censorious creature in the world, and so, I see, it's in vain to 85
talk with you. Pray, will you go back to the company?

LADY EASY.

Ah! Poor Lady Betty!

LADY BETTY MODISH.

Pshaw!   *Exeunt.*

[V.ii]   *The scene changes to* Sir Charles's *Lodgings.*
              Enter Sir Charles *and* Lord Morelove.

LORD MORELOVE.

Charles! You have transported me; you have made my part in the scene so very easy, too. 'Tis impossible I should fail in it.

SIR CHARLES EASY.

That's what I considered, for now the more you throw yourself into her power, the more I shall be able to force 5
her into yours.

LORD MORELOVE.

After all (begging the ladies' pardon), your fine women, like bullies, are only stout where they know their men. A man of honest courage may fright 'em into anything! Well, I am fully instructed and will about it instantly. Won't 10
you go along with me?

SIR CHARLES EASY.

That may not be so proper; besides, I have a little business upon my hands.

LORD MORELOVE.

Oh, your servant, sir! Goodbye to you—you shan't stir.

SIR CHARLES EASY.

My lord, your servant!   *Exit* Lord Morelove. 15
So! Now to dispose of myself till 'tis time to think of my Lady Graveairs. —Umph! I have no great maw to that

[V.i]   [V.ii]
88. Pshaw!] *Q 1–2; om. P.*   12. besides] *P; beside Q 1–2.*

business, methinks. I don't find myself in humor enough to come up to the civil things that are usually expected in the making up of an old quarrel. (Edging *crosses the stage*.) 20
There goes a warmer temptation by half. Ha! Into my wife's bedchamber, too! I question if the jade has any great business there. I have a great fancy she has only a mind to be taking the opportunity of nobody's being at home to make her peace with me. Let me see—ay, I shall have 25
time enough to go to her ladyship afterwards. Besides, I want a little sleep, I find. Your young fops may talk of their women of quality, but to me, now, there's a strange agreeable convenience in a creature one is not obliged to say much to upon these occasions.   *Going.* 30

Enter Edging.

EDGING.

Did you call me, sir?

SIR CHARLES EASY (*aside*).

Ha! All's right. —Yes, madam, I did call you.

EDGING.

What would you please to have, sir?   *He sits down.*

SIR CHARLES EASY.

Have! Why I would have you grow a good girl and know when you are well used, hussy.   35

EDGING.

I don't complain of anything, not I.

SIR CHARLES EASY.

Well, don't be uneasy; I am not angry with you. Now— come and kiss me.

EDGING.

Lard, sir—

SIR CHARLES EASY.

Don't be a fool, now; come hither.   40

EDGING.

Pshaw!   *Goes to him.*

SIR CHARLES EASY.

No wry faces—so—sit down. I won't have you look grave, neither. Let me see you smile, you jade, you.

23. great] *Q 1–2*; *om. P.*   33. S.D. *He sits down*] *Q 1–2*; *Sits*
26. Besides] *P*; Beside *Q 1–2*.   *down. P.*

EDGING.

Ha, ha!   *Laughs and blushes.*

SIR CHARLES EASY.

Ah! You melting rogue!   45

EDGING.

Come, don't you be at your tricks, now! Lard! Can't you
sit still and talk with one? I am sure there's ten times more
love in that, and fifty times the satisfaction, people may say
what they will.

SIR CHARLES EASY.

Well! Now you're good you shall have your own way. I am   50
going to lie down in the next room, and since you love a
little chat, come and throw my nightgown over me, and you
shall talk me to sleep.   *Exit* Sir Charles.

EDGING.

Yes, sir. —For all his way, I see he likes me still.

Exit after him.

[V.iii]   *The scene changes to the Terrace.*
            Enter Lady Betty, Lady Easy, *and* Lord Morelove.

LORD MORELOVE.

Nay, madam, there you are too severe upon him, for bating
now and then a little vanity, my Lord Foppington does not
want wit sometimes to make him a very tolerable woman's
man.

LADY BETTY MODISH.

But such eternal vanity grows tiresome.   5

LADY EASY.

Come, if he were not so loose in his morals, vanity, methinks,
might easily be excused, considering how much 'tis in
fashion. For pray observe, what's half the conversation of
most of the fine young people about town but a perpetual
affectation of appearing foremost in the knowledge of   10
manners, new modes, and scandal, and in that I don't see
anybody comes up to him.

LORD MORELOVE.

Nor I, indeed—and here he comes.— [*To* Lady Betty.]
Pray, madam, let's have a little more of him. Nobody shows
him to more advantage than your ladyship.   15

LADY BETTY MODISH.

Nay, with all my heart. You'll second me, my lord.

LORD MORELOVE.

Upon occasion, madam.

LADY EASY (*aside and smiling to* Lord Morelove).

Engaging upon parties, my lord?

Enter Lord Foppington.

LORD FOPPINGTON.

So, ladies! What's the affair now?

LADY BETTY MODISH.

Why, you were, my lord. I was allowing you a great many   20
good qualities, but Lady Easy says you are a perfect hypocrite, and that whatever airs you give yourself to the
women, she's confident you value no woman in the world
equal to your own lady.

LORD FOPPINGTON [*aside to* Lady Betty].

You see, madam, how I am scandalized upon your account.   25
But it's so natural for a prude to be malicious when a man
endeavors to be well with anybody but herself. Did you
never observe she was piqued at that before? Ha, ha!

LADY BETTY MODISH [*to* Lord Foppington].

I'll swear you are a provoking creature.

LORD FOPPINGTON [*to* Lady Betty].

Let's be more familiar upon't and give her disorder. Ha, ha!   30

LADY BETTY MODISH.

Ha, ha, ha!

LORD FOPPINGTON.

Stap my breath, but Lady Easy is an admirable discoverer.
Marriage is indeed a prodigious security of one's inclination.
A man's likely to take a world of pains in an employment
where he can't be turned out for his idleness.   35

LADY BETTY MODISH.

I vow, my lord, that's vastly generous to all the fine women;
you are for giving 'em a despotic power in love, I see, to reward and punish as they think fit.

LORD FOPPINGTON.

Ha, ha! Right, madam! What signifies beauty without
power? And a fine woman when she's married makes as ridic-   40
ulous a figure as a beaten general marching out of a garrison.

LADY EASY.

I'm afraid, Lady Betty, the greatest danger in your use of
power would be from a too heedless liberality; you would
more mind the man than his merit.

LORD FOPPINGTON (*to* Lady Betty).

Piqued again, by all that's fretful! Well, certainly, to give   45
envy is a pleasure inexpressible.

LADY BETTY MODISH.

Ha, ha, ha!

LADY EASY (*aside to* Lord Morelove).

Does not she show him well, my lord?

LORD MORELOVE (*to* Lady Easy).

Perfectly, and me too, to myself, for now I almost blush
to think I ever was uneasy at him.   50

LORD FOPPINGTON.

Ha, ha! Lady Easy, I ask ten thousand pardons. I'm
afraid I am rude all this while.

LADY EASY.

Oh, not at all, my lord. You are always good company
when you please; not but in some things, indeed, you are
apt to be like other fine gentlemen, a little too loose in your 55
principles.

LORD FOPPINGTON.

Oh, madam! Never to the offense of the ladies. I agree in
any community with them; nobody is a more constant
churchman, when the fine women are there.

LADY EASY.

Oh fie, my lord! You ought not to go for their sakes at all.   60
And I wonder you, that are for being such a good husband
of your virtues, are not afraid of bringing your prudence
into a lampoon or a play.

LADY BETTY MODISH.

Lampoons and plays, madam, are only things to be laughed
at.   65

LORD MORELOVE.

Plays now, indeed, one need not be so much afraid of,
for since the late short-sighted view of 'em vice may go on

51. Ha, ha!] *Q 1–2; om. P.*   66. one] *Q 1–2; we P.*

67. *short-sighted view*] Jeremy Collier's *Short View of the Immorality and
Profaneness of the English Stage* appeared in 1698.

-95-

and prosper; the stage dares hardly show a vicious person speaking like himself for fear of being called profane for exposing him. 70

LADY EASY.

'Tis hard, indeed, when people won't distinguish between what's meant for contempt and what for example.

LORD FOPPINGTON.

Od so! Ladies, the court's coming home, I see. Shall not we go make our bows?

LADY BETTY MODISH.

Oh, by all means! 75

LADY EASY.

Lady Betty, I must leave you, for I'm obliged to write letters, and I know you won't give me time after supper.

LADY BETTY MODISH.

Well, my dear, I'll make a short visit and be with you.

Exit Lady Easy.

Pray, what's become of my Lady Graveairs?

LORD MORELOVE.

I believe she's gone home, madam. She seemed not to be 80 very well.

LORD FOPPINGTON.

And where's Sir Charles, my lord?

LORD MORELOVE.

I left him at his own lodgings.

LADY BETTY MODISH.

He's upon some ramble, I'm afraid.

LORD FOPPINGTON.

Nay, as for that matter, a man may ramble at home 85 sometimes! But here come the chaises. We must make a little more haste, madam. *Exeunt.*

[V.iv] *The scene changes to* Sir Charles's *lodgings.*
Enter Lady Easy *and a* Servant.

LADY EASY.

Is your master come home?

SERVANT.

Yes, madam.

80. I] *Q 1–2*; Oh I *P.*

LADY EASY.

    Where is he?

SERVANT.

    I believe, madam, he's laid down to sleep.

LADY EASY.

    Where's Edging? Bid her get me some wax and paper—   5
stay! It's no matter, now I think on it, there's some above
upon my toilet.   *Exeunt severally.*

[V.v]

The scene opens and discovers Sir Charles *without his periwig and* Edging
by him, both asleep in two easy chairs. And then enter Lady Easy, *who starts
and trembles some time, unable to speak.*

LADY EASY.

    Ha!
    Protect me virtue, patience, reason!
    Teach me to bear this killing sight, or let
    Me think my dreaming senses are deceived!
    For sure a sight like this might raise the arm   5
    Of duty, even to the breast of love. At least
    I'll throw this vizor of my patience off,
    Now wake him in his guilt,
    And barefaced front him with my wrongs.
    I'll talk to him till he blushes, nay till he   10
    Frowns on me, perhaps—and then
    I'm lost again. The ease of a few tears
    Is all that's left to me—
    And duty, too, forbids me to insult
    Where I have vowed obedience. Perhaps   15
    The fault's in me, and nature has not formed
    Me with the thousand little requisites
    That warm the heart to love.
    Somewhere there is a fault,
    But heaven best knows what both of us deserve.   20
    Ha! Bareheaded and in so sound a sleep!
    Who knows, while thus exposed to the unwholesome air,

[V.iv]
6. on it] *Q 1–2*; on't *P.*

[V.v]
0.2. *And then*] *Q 1–2*; *Then P.*
22. the unwholesome] *Q 1–2*; th'
unwholesome *P.*

But heaven, offended, may o'ertake his crime,
And, in some languishing distemper, leave him
A severe example of its violated laws.   25
Forbid it mercy, and forbid it love!
This may prevent it.

Takes a steinkirk from her neck and lays it gently over his head.

And if he should wake offended at my too-busy care, let
my heart-breaking patience, duty, and my fond affection
plead my pardon.   *Exit.*   30

*After she has been out some time, a bell rings; at which the maid, waking,
starts and stirs Sir Charles.*

EDGING.

Oh!

SIR CHARLES EASY.

How now! What's the matter?

EDGING.

Oh, bless my soul! My lady's come home.

SIR CHARLES EASY.

Go! Go then!

EDGING.

O lud! My head's in such a condition, too.   (*Runs to the*   35
glass. Bell rings.)   I am coming, madam. —O lud! Here's
no powder neither—here madam!   *Exit.*

SIR CHARLES EASY.

How now!   (*Feeling the steinkirk upon his head.*)   What's
this? How came it here? Did not I see my wife wear this
today? —Death! She can't have been here, sure! It could   40
not be jealousy that brought her home, for my coming was
accidental; so too, I fear, might hers. How careless have I
been! Not to secure the door neither!— 'twas foolish. It must

23–27.] P; *prose in* Q 1–2.
25. its] P; *his* Q 1–2.
27.1. *from*] Q 1–2; *off* P.
27.1 *over*] Q 1–2; *on* P.
30.1–2. *at* ... Charles] Q 1–2;
Edging *wakes and stirs* Sir Charles. P.

35–36. S.D. *Runs . . . rings*] *in* Q 1–2
S.D. *applies to* Sir Charles.
39. here?] Q 1–2; here? (*Puts on his
wig.*) P.

27.1. *steinkirk*] a French neckcloth named after the site of a French
victory over the English in 1692.

be so! She certainly has seen me here sleeping with her
woman. If so, how low an hypocrite to her must that sight   45
have proved me! The thought has made me despicable ev'n
to myself. How mean a vice is lying! and how often have
these empty pleasures lulled my honor and my conscience
to a lethargy, while I grossly have abused her, poorly
skulking behind a thousand falsehoods. Now I reflect, this   50
has not been the first of her discoveries. How contemptible
a figure must I have made to her! A crowd of recollected
circumstances confirm me now, she has been long acquainted
with my follies, and yet with what amazing prudence has she
borne the secret pangs of injured love, and wore an ever-   55
lasting smile to me! This asks a little thinking; something
should be done. I'll see her instantly, and be resolved from
her behavior.   *Exit.*

[V.vi]   *The scene changes to another room.*
                         Enter Lady Easy *and* Edging.

LADY EASY.
   Where have you been, Edging?
EDGING.
   Been, madam? I—I—I came as soon as I heard you ring,
   madam.
LADY EASY (*aside*).
   How guilt confounds her! But she's below my thought.
   —Fetch my last new scarf hither. I have a mind to alter it   5
   a little; make haste.
EDGING.
   Yes, madam.—   [*Aside.*]   I see she does not suspect any-
   thing.   *Exit.*
LADY EASY (*sitting down*).
   Heigh ho! I had forgot—but I'm unfit for writing now.
   'Twas an hard conflict, yet it's a joy to think it over, a   10
   secret pride to tell my heart my conduct has been just.
   How low are vicious minds that offer injuries, how much
   superior innocence that bears 'em? Still, there's a pleasure
   ev'n in the melancholy of a quiet conscience. Away, my

2. I—I—I] Q *1–2;* I—I—I—I *P.*

tears! It is not yet impossible, for while his humane nature   15
is not quite shook off, I ought not to despair.

Re-enter Edging *with a scarf.*

EDGING.

Here's the scarf, madam.

LADY EASY.

So, sit down there and—let me see—here, rip off all that
silver.

EDGING.

Indeed, I always thought it would become your ladyship   20
better without it. But now suppose, madam, you carried
another row of gold round those scallops, and then you take
and lay this silver plain all along the gathers, and your
ladyship will perfectly see, it will give the thing ten thousand
times another air.   25

LADY EASY.

Prithee, don't be impertinent, do as I bid you.

EDGING.

Nay, madam, with all my heart. Your ladyship may do
as you please.

LADY EASY (*aside*).

This creature grows so confident, and I dare not part
with her lest he should think it jealousy.   30

Enter Sir Charles.

SIR CHARLES EASY.

So, my dear! What, at work? How are you employed,
pray?

LADY EASY.

I was thinking to alter this scarf here.

SIR CHARLES EASY.

What's amiss? Methinks it's very pretty.

EDGING.

Yes, sir, it's pretty enough, for that matter, but my lady   35
had a mind it should be proper, too.

15. tears] *Q 1–2*; fears *P*.   36. had] *Q 1–2*; has *P*.
22. those] *Q 1–2*; the *P*.

SIR CHARLES EASY.

Indeed!

LADY EASY.

I fancy plain gold and black would become me better.

SIR CHARLES EASY.

That's a grave thought, my dear.

EDGING.

Oh, dear sir, not at all! My lady's much in the right. I   40
am sure, as it is, it's fit for nothing but a girl.

SIR CHARLES EASY.

Leave the room.

EDGING.

Lard, sir! I can't stir, I must stay to—

SIR CHARLES EASY (*angrily*).

Go!

EDGING (*throwing down the scarf hastily and crying aside*).

If ever I speak to him again I'll be burned.   *Exit* Edging.   45

SIR CHARLES EASY.

Sit still, my dear. I came to talk with you, and—which you
may well wonder at—what I have to say is of importance,
too, but 'tis in order to my hereafter always talking kindly
to you.

LADY EASY.

Your words were never disobliging, nor can I charge you   50
with a look that ever had the appearance of unkind.

SIR CHARLES EASY.

The perpetual spring of your good humor lets me draw no
merit from what I have appeared to be, which makes me
curious now to know your thoughts of what I really am.
And never having asked you this before, it puzzles me, nor   55
can I (that strange negligence considered) reconcile to
reason your first thoughts of venturing upon marriage with
me.

LADY EASY.

I never thought it such an hazard.

SIR CHARLES EASY.

How could a woman of your restraint in principles, sedate-   60
ness, sense, and tender disposition propose to see an happy

---

45. S.D. *scarf*] *Q 1–2*; *work P.*   56. that] *Q 1–2*; *om. P.*

life with one (now I reflect) that hardly took an hour's pains, ev'n before marriage, to appear but what I am—a loose, unheeding wretch, absent in all I do, civil, and as often rude without design, unseasonably thoughtful, easy to a fault, and 65 in my best of praise but carelessly good-natured. How shall I reconcile your temper with having made so strange a choice?

LADY EASY.

Your own words may answer you—your having never seemed to be but what you really were, and through that 70 carelessness of temper, there still shone forth to me an undesigning honesty I always doubted of in smoother faces. Thus, while I saw you took least pains to win me, you pleased and wooed me most. Nay, I have often thought that such a temper could never be deliberately unkind, or, 75 at the worst, I knew that errors from want of thinking might be borne, at least when probably one moment's serious thought would end 'em. These were my worst of fears, and these, when weighed by growing love against my solid hopes, were nothing.   80

SIR CHARLES EASY.

My dear, your understanding startles me, and justly calls my own in question. I blush to think I've worn so bright a jewel in my bosom and till this hour have scarce been curious once to look upon its luster.

LADY EASY.

You set too high a value on the common qualities of an 85 easy wife.

SIR CHARLES EASY.

Virtues, like benefits, are double when concealed, and I confess I yet suspect you of an higher value far than I have spoke you.

LADY EASY.

I understand you not.   90

SIR CHARLES EASY.

I'll speak more plainly to you. Be free and tell me—where did you leave this handkerchief?

LADY EASY.

Hah!

SIR CHARLES EASY.

What is't you start at? You hear the question.

LADY EASY.

What shall I say? My fears confound me. 95

SIR CHARLES EASY.

Be not concerned, my dear. Be easy in the truth and tell me.

LADY EASY.

I cannot speak—and I could wish you'd not oblige me to it. 'Tis the only thing I ever yet refused you, and though I want a reason for my will, let me not answer you.

SIR CHARLES EASY.

Your will then be a reason, and since I see you are so 100 generously tender of reproaching me, 'tis fit I should be easy in my gratitude, and make what ought to be my shame my joy. Let me be therefore pleased to tell you now, your wondrous conduct has waked me to a sense of your disquiet past, and resolution never to disturb it more. And (not 105 that I offer it as a merit, but yet in blind compliance to my will) let me beg you would immediately discharge your woman.

LADY EASY.

Alas! I think not of her. Oh, my dear! Distract me not with this excess of goodness. *Weeping.* 110

SIR CHARLES EASY.

Nay, praise me not, lest I reflect how little I have deserved it. I see you are in pain to give me this confusion. Come, I will not shock your softness by my untimely blush for what is past, but rather soothe you to a pleasure at my sense of joy for my recovered happiness to come. Give then to my 115 new-born love what name you please, it cannot, shall not, be too kind—oh! it cannot be too soft for what my soul swells up with emulation to deserve. Receive me then entire at last, and take what yet no woman ever truly had, my conquered heart. 120

LADY EASY.

Oh, the soft treasure! Oh, the dear reward of long desiring love! Now I am blessed indeed to see you kind without the expense of pain in being so, to make you mine with easiness thus! Thus to have you mine is something more than happiness, 'tis double life, and madness of abounding joy. 125 But 'twas pain intolerable to give you a confusion.

103. me be] *P*; me *Q 1–2.*

SIR CHARLES EASY.

Oh, thou engaging virtue! But I'm too slow in doing justice
to thy love. I know thy softness will refuse me, but remember
I insist upon it; let thy woman be discharged this minute.

LADY EASY.

No, my dear, think me not so low in faith, to fear that, 130
after what you've said, 'twill ever be in her power to do
me future injury. When I can conveniently provide for her
I'll think on't, but to discharge her now might let her guess
at the occasion, and methinks I would have all our differen-
ces, like our endearments, be equally a secret to our servants. 135

SIR CHARLES EASY.

Still my superior every way. Be it as you have better
thought. Well, my dear, now I'll confess a thing that was not
in your power to accuse me of. To be short, I own this
creature is not the only one I have been to blame with.

LADY EASY.

I know she is not, and was always less concerned to find it 140
so, for constancy in errors might have been fatal to me.

SIR CHARLES EASY (*surprised*).

What is it you know, my dear?

LADY EASY.

Come, I am not afraid to accuse you now—my Lady
Graveairs. Your carelessness, my dear, let all the world
know it, and it would have been hard indeed had it been 145
only to me a secret.

SIR CHARLES EASY.

My dear, I'll ask no more questions for fear of being more
ridiculous. I do confess, I thought my discretion there had
been a masterpiece. How contemptible must I have
looked all this while!
                                                      150

LADY EASY.

You shan't say so.

SIR CHARLES EASY.

Well, to let you see I had some shame as well as nature
in me, I had writ this to my Lady Graveairs upon my
first discovering that you knew I had wronged you. Read
it.
                                                      155

LADY EASY (*reads*).

"Something has happened that prevents the visit I intended

you, and I could gladly wish you never would reproach
me if I tell you 'tis utterly inconvenient that I should ever
see you more." This, indeed, was more than I had merited.

Enter a Servant.

SIR CHARLES EASY.

Who's there? Here, step with this to my Lady Graveairs. 160
                    Seals the letter and gives it to the Servant.

SERVANT.

Yes, sir. —Madam, my Lady Betty's come.

LADY EASY.

I'll wait on her.   [*Exit* Servant.]

SIR CHARLES EASY.

My dear, I'm thinking there may be other things my
negligency may have wronged you in; but be assured, as I
discover 'em, all shall be corrected. Is there any part or 165
circumstance in your fortune that I can change or yet
make easier to you?

LADY EASY.

None, my dear. Your good nature never stinted me in
that, and now, methinks, I have less occasion than ever.

Re-enter Servant.

SERVANT.

Sir, my Lord Morelove's come.   170

SIR CHARLES EASY.

I am coming.   [*Exit* Servant.]
I think I told you of the design we had laid against Lady
Betty.

LADY EASY.

You did, and I should be pleased to be myself concerned in
it.   175

SIR CHARLES EASY.

I believe we may employ you. I know he waits me with
impatience. But, my dear, won't you think me tasteless
to the joy you've given me, to suffer at this time any concern but you t'employ my thoughts?

LADY EASY.

Seasons must be obeyed, and since I know your friend's 180
happiness depending, I could not taste my own should you
neglect it.

SIR CHARLES EASY.

Thou easy sweetness! Oh, what a waste on thy neglected
love has my unthinking brain committed! But time and
future thrift of tenderness shall yet repair it all. The hours 185
will come when this soft gliding stream that swells my
heart uninterrupted shall renew its course,
            And like the ocean after ebb, shall move
            With constant force of due returning love.   *Exeunt.*

[V.vii]   *The scene changes to another room.*
              And then re-enter Lady Easy *and* Lady Betty.

LADY BETTY MODISH.

You've been in tears, my dear, and yet you look pleased
too.

LADY EASY.

You'll pardon me if I can't yet let you into circumstances,
but be satisfied Sir Charles has made me happy ev'n to a
pain of joy.   5

LADY BETTY MODISH.

Indeed, I am truly glad of it, though I am sorry to find
that anyone who has generosity enough to do you justice
should unprovoked be so great an enemy to me.

LADY EASY.

Sir Charles your enemy!

LADY BETTY MODISH.

My dear, you'll pardon me if I always thought him so. 10
But now I am convinced of it.

LADY EASY.

In what, pray? I can't think you'll find him so.

LADY BETTY MODISH.

Oh, madam! It has been his whole business of late to make
an utter breach between my Lord Morelove and me.

LADY EASY.

That may be owing to your usage of my lord. Perhaps he 15
thought it would not disoblige you. I am confident you are
mistaken in him.

1. You've] *Q 1–2*; You have *P.*   3. let] *Q 1–2*; *om. P.*

LADY BETTY MODISH.

Oh, I don't use to be out in things of this nature. I can
see well enough. But I shall be able to tell you more when I
have talked with my lord. Ha, ha, ha!   20

LADY EASY.

Here he comes, and because you shall talk with him—no
excuses—for positively I will leave you together.

LADY BETTY MODISH.

Indeed, my dear, I desire you would stay then, for I know
you think now that I have a mind to—to—

LADY EASY.

To—to—ha, ha, ha!   *Going.*   25

LADY BETTY MODISH.

Well! Remember this!

Enter Lord Morelove.

LORD MORELOVE.

I hope I don't fright you away, madam.

LADY EASY.

Not at all, my lord. But I must beg your pardon for a
moment. I'll wait upon you immediately.   *Exit.*

LADY BETTY MODISH.

My Lady Easy gone?   30

LORD MORELOVE.

Perhaps, madam, in friendship to you she thinks I may
have deserved the coldness you of late have shown me, and
was willing to give you this opportunity to convince me you
have not done it without just grounds and reason.

LADY BETTY MODISH (*aside*).

How handsomely does he reproach me! But I can't bear   35
that he should think I know it. —My lord, whatever has
passed between you and me, I dare swear that could not be
her thought at this time, for when two people have appeared
professed enemies, she can't but think one will as little care
to give, as t'other to receive, a justification of their actions. 40

LORD MORELOVE.

Passion indeed often does repented injuries on both sides,
but I don't remember in my heat of error I ever yet professed myself your enemy.

20. Ha, ha, ha!] *Q 1–2*; *om. P.*   22. I will] *Q 1–2*; I'll *P.*

LADY BETTY MODISH.

My lord, I shall be very free with you. I confess I do think
now I have not a greater enemy in the world.   45

LORD MORELOVE.

If having long loved you, to my own disquiet, be injurious,
I am contented then to stand the foremost of your enemies.

LADY BETTY MODISH.

Oh, my lord, there's no great fear of your being my enemy
that way, I dare say.

LORD MORELOVE.

There is no other way my heart can bear to offend you now,   50
and I foresee in that it will persist to my undoing.

LADY BETTY MODISH.

Fie, fie, my lord! We know where your heart is well
enough.

LORD MORELOVE.

My conduct has indeed deserved this scorn, and therefore
'tis but just I should submit to your resentment, and beg   55
(though I'm assured in vain) for pardon.   *Kneels.*

Enter Sir Charles.

SIR CHARLES EASY.

How, my lord!   Lord Morelove *rises.*

LADY BETTY MODISH (*aside*).

Ha! He here? This was unlucky.

LORD MORELOVE (*to* Lady Betty).

Oh, pity my confusion!

SIR CHARLES EASY.

I am sorry to see you can so soon forget yourself; methinks   60
the insults you have borne from that lady, by this time,
should have warned you into a disgust of her regardless
principles.

LORD MORELOVE.

Hold, Sir Charles! While you and I are friends I desire
you would speak with honor of this lady. 'Tis sufficient I   65
have no complaint against her, and—

LADY BETTY MODISH.

My lord, I beg you would resent this thing no farther. An

50. There is] *Q 1–2*; There's *P.*   56. I'm] *Q 1–2*; I am *P.*

injury like this is better punished with our contempt.
Apparent malice only should be laughed at.

SIR CHARLES EASY.

Ha, ha! The old recourse! Offers of any hopes to delude   70
him from his resentment, and then, as the Grand Monarch
did with the Cavalier, you are sure to keep your word
with him.

LADY BETTY MODISH.

Sir Charles, to let you know how far I am above your little
spleen, my lord, your hand from this hour!   75

SIR CHARLES EASY.

Pshaw! pshaw! All design! all pique! mere artifice and
disappointed woman.

LADY BETTY MODISH.

Look you, sir, not that I doubt my lord's opinion of me,
yet—

SIR CHARLES EASY.

Look you, madam! In short, your word has been too often   80
taken to let you make up quarrels, as you used to do, with a
soft look and a fair promise you never intended to keep.

LADY BETTY MODISH.

Was ever such an insolence! He won't give me leave to
speak.

LORD MORELOVE.

Sir Charles!   85

LADY BETTY MODISH.

No, pray, my lord, have patience, and since his malice seems
to grow particular, I dare his worst and urge him to the
proof on't. Pray, sir, wherein can you charge me with breach
of promise to my lord?

SIR CHARLES EASY.

Death! You won't deny it? How often, to piece up a quarrel,   90
have you appointed him to visit you alone, and though you
have promised to see no other company the whole day, when
he has come he has found you among the laugh of noisy fops,

71–72. *Grand . . . Cavalier*] Jean Cavalier, leader of the Camisards, was in
1704 bribed by Louis XIV to make peace with him. Deserted by his
disillusioned troops, Cavalier, it was rumored, was in danger of being
imprisoned by Louis.

coquettes, and coxcombs, dissolutely gay, while your full
eyes ran o'er with transport of their flattery and your own   95
vain power of pleasing? How often, I say, have you been
known to throw away at least four hours of your good humor
upon such wretches, and the minute they were gone, grew
only dull to him, sunk into a distasteful spleen, complained
you had talked yourself into the headache, and then indulged 100
upon the dear delight of seeing him in pain. And by that
time you stretched and gaped him heartily out of patience,
of a sudden most importunately remember you had outsat
your appointment with my Lady Fiddle-faddle, and immediately order your coach to the park.   105

LADY BETTY MODISH.

Yet, sir, have you done?

SIR CHARLES EASY.

No—though this might serve to show the nature of your
principles. But the noble conquest you have gained at last,
over defeated sense of reputation, too, has made your fame
immortal.   110

LORD MORELOVE.

How, sir?

LADY BETTY MODISH.

My reputation?

SIR CHARLES EASY.

Ay, madam, your reputation. My lord, if I advance a falsehood, then resent it. I say, your reputation; 't has been your
life's whole pride of late to be the common toast of every   115
public table, vain even in the infamous addresses of a
married man, my Lord Foppington; let that be reconciled
with reputation, I'll now shake hands with shame and bow
me to the low contempt which you deserve from him. Not but
I suppose you'll yet endeavor to recover him. Now you   120
find ill usage in danger of losing your conquest, 'tis possible
you'll stop at nothing to preserve it.

LADY BETTY MODISH.

Sir Charles—   *Walks disordered, and he after her.*

102. you] *Q 1–2*; you had *P*.   103. importunately] *P*; importantly
                                         Q 1–2.

SIR CHARLES EASY.

    I know your vanity is so voracious 'twill ev'n wound itself
to feed itself—offer him a blank, perhaps, to fill up with 125
hopes of what nature he pleases, and part with ev'n your
pride to keep him on.

LADY BETTY MODISH (*bursting into tears*).

    Sir Charles, I have not deserved this of you.

SIR CHARLES EASY.

    Ah! True woman! Drop him a soft, dissembling tear, and
then his just resentment must be hushed, of course.   130

LORD MORELOVE.

    O Charles! I can bear no more. Those tears are too re-
proaching.

SIR CHARLES (*aside, and then aloud*).

    Hist for your life! —My lord, if you believe her you're
undone. The very next sight of my Lord Foppington would
make her yet forswear all that she can promise.   135

LADY BETTY MODISH.

    My Lord Foppington! Is that the mighty crime that must
condemn me then? You know I used him but as a tool of
my resentment, which you yourself, by a pretended friendship to us both, most artfully provoked me to.

LORD MORELOVE.

    Hold, I conjure you, madam! I want not this conviction.   140

LADY BETTY MODISH.

    Send for him this minute, and you and he shall both be
witnesses of the contempt and detestation I have for any
forward hopes his vanity may have given him or your malice
would insinuate.

SIR CHARLES EASY.

    Death! You would as soon eat fire, as soon part with your 145
luxurious taste of folly, as dare to own the half before his
face, or any one, that would make you blush to deny it to.
—Here comes my wife. Now we shall see. —Ha, and my
Lord Foppington with her! —Now, now, we shall see this
mighty proof of your sincerity. —Now, my lord, you'll have 150
a warning, sure, and henceforth know me for your friend
indeed.

149. we] *Q 1–2*; you *P.*

Enter Lady Easy *and* Lord Foppington.

LADY EASY.

    In tears, my dear? What the matter?

LADY BETTY MODISH.

    Oh, my dear, all I told you's true. Sir Charles has shown
himself so inveterately my enemy that if I believed I de- 155
served but half his hate, 'twould make me hate myself.

LORD FOPPINGTON.

    Hark you, Charles! Prithee what is this business?

SIR CHARLES EASY.

    Why yours, my lord, for aught I know. I have made such
a breach betwixt 'em—I can't promise much for the
courage of a woman, but if hers holds, I am sure it's wide 160
enough, you may enter ten abreast, my lord.

LORD FOPPINGTON.

    Say'st thou so, Charles? Then I hold six to four I am the
first man in town.

LADY EASY.

    Sure, there must be some mistake in this. I hope he has
not made my lord your enemy.   165

LADY BETTY MODISH.

    I know not what he has done.

LORD MORELOVE.

    Far be that thought! Alas! I am too much in fear myself
that what I have this day committed, advised by his mistaken friendship, may have done my love irreparable
prejudice.   170

LADY BETTY MODISH.

    No, my lord. Since I perceive his little arts have not pre-
vailed upon your good nature to my prejudice, I am
bound in gratitude, in duty to myself, and to the con-
fession you have made, my lord, to acknowledge now
I have been to blame too.   175

LORD MORELOVE.

    Ha! Is't possible? Can you own so much? Oh, my trans-
ported heart!

155. inveterately] *Q 1–2*; inveter-
ably *P.*

LADY BETTY MODISH.

He says I have taken pleasure in seeing you uneasy. I
own it, but 'twas when that uneasiness, I thought, proceeded from your love; and if you did love—'twill not   180
be much to pardon it.

LORD MORELOVE.

Oh, let my soul, thus bending to your power, adore this
soft descending goodness.

LADY BETTY MODISH.

And since the giddy woman's slights I have shown you too
often have been public, 'tis fit at last th' amends and repara-   185
tion should be so: therefore, what I offered to Sir Charles,
I now repeat before this company, my utter detestation of
any past or future gallantry that has or shall be offered me to
your uneasiness.

LORD MORELOVE.

Oh, be less generous, or teach me to deserve it. —Now   190
blush, Sir Charles, at your injurious accusation.

LORD FOPPINGTON (aside).

Hah! *Pardi, voilà quelque chose d'extraordinaire.*

LADY BETTY MODISH.

As for my Lord Foppington, I owe him thanks for having
been so friendly an instrument of our reconciliation; for
though in the little outward gallantry I received from   195
him I did not immediately trust him with my design in it,
yet I have a better opinion of his understanding than to
suppose he could mistake it.

LORD FOPPINGTON [aside].

I am struck dumb with the deliberation of her assurance,
and do not positively remember that the nonchalance of my   200
temper ever had so bright an occasion to show itself before.

LADY BETTY MODISH.

My lord, I hope you'll pardon the freedom I have taken
with you.

LORD FOPPINGTON.

Oh, madam, don't be under the confusion of an apology
upon my account, for in cases of this nature I am never   205
disappointed but when I find the lady of the same mind

185. been] *Q 1–2*; been made *P.*   199. the] *Q 1–2*; *om. P.*

two hours together. Madam, I have lost a thousand fine
women in my time, but never had the ill manners to be
out of humor with any one for refusing me since I was born.

LADY BETTY MODISH.

My lord, that's a very prudent temper.   210

LORD FOPPINGTON.

Madam, to convince you that I am in a universal peace
with mankind, since you own I have so far contributed
to your happiness, give me leave to have the honor of
completing it by joining your hand where you have already
offered up your inclination.   215

LADY BETTY MODISH.

My lord, that's a favor I can't refuse you.

LORD MORELOVE.

Generous indeed, my lord.

                              Lord Foppington *joins their hands.*

LORD FOPPINGTON.

And stap my breath if ever I was better pleased since my
first entrance into human nature.

SIR CHARLES EASY.

How now, my lord! What! Throw up your cards before   220
you have lost the game?

LORD FOPPINGTON.

Look you, Charles, 'tis true I did design to have played with
her alone, but he that will keep well with the ladies must
sometimes be content to make one at a pool with 'em, and
since I know I must engage her in my turn, I don't see any   225
great odds in letting him take the first game with her.

SIR CHARLES EASY.

Wisely considered, my lord.

LADY BETTY MODISH.

And now, Sir Charles—

SIR CHARLES EASY.

And now, madam, I'll save you the trouble of a long
speech, and, in one word, confess that everything I have   230
done in regard to you this day was purely artificial. I saw
there was no way to secure you to my Lord Morelove but
by alarming your pride with the danger of losing him, and

211. a] *Q 1–2*; an *P.*   220. your] *Q 1–2*; the *P.*

since the success must have by this time convinced you that
in love nothing is more ridiculous than an over-acted 235
aversion, I am sure you won't take it ill if we at last con-
gratulate your good nature by heartily laughing at the
fright we had put you in. Ha, ha, ha!

LADY EASY.

Ha, ha, ha!

LADY BETTY MODISH.

Why—well, I declare it now, I hate you worse than ever.   240

SIR CHARLES EASY.

Ha, ha, ha! And was it afraid they would take its love
from it? Poor Lady Betty! Ha, ha!

LADY EASY.

My dear, I beg your pardon, but 'tis impossible not to
laugh when one's so heartily pleased.

LORD FOPPINGTON.

Really, madam, I am afraid the good humor of the com- 245
pany will draw me into your displeasure too, but if I
were to expire at this moment, my last breath would positively go out in a laugh. Ha, ha, ha!

LADY BETTY MODISH.

Nay, I have deserved it all, that's the truth on't.— [*To*
Lord Morelove.]   But I hope, my lord, you were not in 250
this design against me.

LORD MORELOVE.

As a proof, madam, I am inclined never to deceive you
more—I do confess, I had my share in't.

LADY BETTY MODISH.

You do, my lord! Then I declare 'twas a design, one or
other, the best carried on that ever I knew in my life, and 255
(to my shame I own it) for aught I know the only thing that
would have prevailed upon my temper. 'Twas a foolish
pride that has cost me many a bitten lip to support it. I
wish we don't both repent, my lord.

LORD MORELOVE.

Don't you repent without me, and we never shall.   260

SIR CHARLES EASY.

Well, madam, now the worst that the world can say of

258. bitten] *P*; bitter *Q 1–2.*

---

your past conduct is that my lord had constancy and you
have tried it.

Enter a Servant *to* Lord Morelove.

SERVANT.

My lord, Mr. Le Fevre's below and desires to know what
time your lordship will please to have the music begin.   265

LORD MORELOVE.

Sir Charles, what say you? Will you give me leave to bring
'em hither?

SIR CHARLES EASY.

As the ladies think fit, my lord.

LADY BETTY MODISH.

Oh, by all means! 'Twill be better here, unless we could
have the terrace to ourselves.   270

LORD MORELOVE.

Then pray desire 'em to come all hither immediately.

SERVANT.

Yes, my lord.   *Exit* Servant.

Enter Lady Graveairs.

SIR CHARLES EASY.

Lady Graveairs!

LADY GRAVEAIRS.

Yes! You may well start! But don't suppose I am now come
like a poor tame fool to upbraid your guilt, but, if I could, 275
to blast you with a look.

SIR CHARLES EASY.

Come, come, you yet have sense. Don't expose yourself.
You are unhappy and I own myself the cause. The only
satisfaction I can offer you is to protest no new engagement
takes me from you, but a sincere reflection of the long neg- 280
lect and injuries I've done the best of wives, for whose
amends and only sake I now must part with you and all the
inconvenient pleasures of my life.

LADY GRAVEAIRS.

Have you, then, fallen into the low contempt of exposing me,
and to your wife, too?   285

277. yet] *Q 1–2; om. P.*   282. now *Q 1–2; om. P.*

SIR CHARLES EASY.

'Twas impossible, without it, I could ever be sincere in my conversion.

LADY GRAVEAIRS.

Despicable!

SIR CHARLES EASY.

Do not think it so; for my sake I know she'll not reproach you, nor by her carriage ever let the world perceive you've 290 wronged her. —My dear—

LADY EASY.

Lady Graveairs, I hope you'll sup with us?

LADY GRAVEAIRS.

I can't refuse so much good company, madam.

SIR CHARLES EASY.

You see the worst of her resentment. In the meantime don't endeavor to be her friend, and she'll never be your 295 enemy.

LADY GRAVEAIRS.

I am unfortunate; 'tis what my folly has deserved, and I submit to it.

LORD MORELOVE.

So! Here's the music.

LADY EASY.

Come, ladies. Shall we sit?   *After the music, a song.* 300

> Sabina with an angel's face
>   By love ordained for joy,
> Seems of the sirens' cruel race,
>   To charm and then destroy.

> With all the arts of look and dress   305
>   She fans the fatal fire,
> Through pride, mistaken oft for grace,
>   She bids the swain expire.

> The god of love, enraged to see
>   The nymph defy his flame,   310
> Pronounced this merciless decree
>   Against the haughty dame.

> Let age with double speed o'ertake her,
>   Let love the room of pride supply,
> And when the lovers all forsake her,   315
>   A spotless virgin let her die.

Sir Charles comes forward with Lady Easy.

SIR CHARLES EASY.

Now, my dear, I find my happiness grow fast upon me.
In all my past experience of the sex I found even among
the better sort so much of folly, pride, malice, passion,
and irresolute desire, that I concluded thee but of the fore- 320
most rank, and therefore scarce worthy my concern. But
thou hast stirred me with so severe a proof of thy exalted
virtue, it gives me wonder equal to my love. If then the
unkindly thought of what I have been hereafter should
intrude upon thy growing quiet, let this reflection teach thee 325
to be easy:

> Thy wrongs, when greatest, most thy virtue proved,
> And from that virtue found, I blushed, and truly loved.

Exeunt.

328.1. *Exeunt.*] *P*; *om. Q 1–2*.

EPILOGUE

Conquest and freedom are at length our own, ⎫
False fears of slavery no more are shown, ⎬
Nor dread of paying tribute to a foreign throne. ⎭
All stations now the fruits of conquest share, ⎫
Except (if small with great things may compare) ⎬ 5
Th'opprest condition of the lab'ring player. ⎭
We're still in fears (as you of late from France) ⎫
Of the despotic power of song and dance. ⎭
For while subscription, like a tyrant reigns, ⎫
Nature's neglected, and the stage in chains, ⎬ 10
And English actors slaves to swell the Frenchman's gains. ⎭
Like Aesop's crow, the poor outwitted stage,
That lived on wholesome plays i'th' latter age,
Deluded once to sing, ev'n justly served,
Let fall her cheese to the fox's mouth and starved. 15
Oh, that your judgment, as your courage has ⎫
Your fame extended, would assert our cause, ⎬
That nothing English might submit to foreign laws. ⎭
If we but live to see that joyful day, ⎫
Then of the English stage, revived, we may, ⎬ 20
As of your honor now, with proper application, say. ⎭

So when the Gallic fox by fraud of peace
Had lulled the British lion into ease,
And saw that sleep composed his couchant head,
He bids him wake and see himself betrayed 25
In toils of treacherous politics around him laid:
Shows him how one close hour of Gallic thought
Retook those towns for which he years had fought.

---

1. *Conquest and freedom*] Marlborough's 1704 campaign culminated in the Battle of Blenheim.

8. *song and dance*] Cibber's displeasure at the invasion by foreign singers and dancers is echoed in the Epistle Dedicatory to *The Lady's Last Stake* (1707).

9. *subscription*] singers and instrumentalists usually performed by subscription.

28. *those towns*] in 1701 various fortresses in the Netherlands were ceded to the French.

-119-

At this th'indignant savage rolls his fiery eyes,
Dauntless, though blushing at the base surprise,   30
Pauses awhile—but finds delays are vain.
Compelled to fight he shakes his shaggy main,
He grinds his dreadful fangs and stalks to Blenheim's plain.
There, with erected crest and horrid roar,
He furious plunges on through streams of gore,   35
And dyes with false Bavarian blood the purple Danube's
   shore.
In one pushed battle frees the destined slaves,
Revives old English honor, and an empire saves.

---

29. *th'indignant savage*] i.e., the British lion.
36. *false Bavarian*] the Bavarians were allied to the French in the War of the Spanish Succession.

Appendix

Chronology

Approximate years are indicated by *.

Political and Literary Events	Life and Major Works of Cibber

1631
Shirley's *THE TRAITOR.*
Death of Donne.
John Dryden born.

1633
Samuel Pepys born.

1635
Sir George Etherege born.*

1640
Aphra Behn born.*

1641
William Wycherley born.*

1642
First Civil War began (ended 1646).
Theaters closed by Parliament.
Thomas Shadwell born.*

1648
Second Civil War.

1649
Execution of Charles I.

1650
Jeremy Collier born.

1651
Hobbes' *Leviathan* published.

1652
First Dutch War began (ended 1654).
Thomas Otway born.

1653
Nathaniel Lee born.*

1656
D'Avenant's *THE SIEGE OF RHODES* performed at Rutland House.

1657
John Dennis born.

1658
Death of Oliver Cromwell.
D'Avenant's *THE CRUELTY OF THE SPANIARDS IN PERU* performed at the Cockpit.

1660
Restoration of Charles II.
Theatrical patents granted to Thomas Killigrew and Sir William D'Avenant, authorizing them to form, respectively, the King's and the Duke of York's Companies.
Pepys began his diary.

1661
Cowley's *THE CUTTER OF COLEMAN STREET*.
D'Avenant's *THE SIEGE OF RHODES* (expanded to two parts).

1662
Charter granted to the Royal Society.

1663
Dryden's *THE WILD GALLANT*.
Tuke's *THE ADVENTURES OF FIVE HOURS*.

1664
Sir John Vanbrugh born.
Dryden's *THE RIVAL LADIES*.
Dryden and Howard's *THE INDIAN QUEEN*.
Etherege's *THE COMICAL REVENGE*.

1665
Second Dutch War began (ended
1667).
Great Plague.
Dryden's *THE INDIAN EM-
PEROR.*
Orrery's *MUSTAPHA.*

1666
Fire of London.
Death of James Shirley.

1667
Milton's *Paradise Lost* published.
Sprat's *The History of the Royal
Society* published.
Dryden's *SECRET LOVE.*

1668
Death of D'Avenant.
Dryden made Poet Laureate.
Dryden's *An Essay of Dramatic
Poesy* published.
Shadwell's *THE SULLEN LOV-
ERS.*

1669
Pepys terminated his diary.
Susannah Centlivre born.

1670
William Congreve born.
Dryden's *THE CONQUEST OF
GRANADA*, Part I.

1671
Dorset Garden Theatre (Duke's   Born in London.
Company) opened.
Milton's *Paradise Regained* and *Sam-
son Agonistes* published.
Dryden's *THE CONQUEST OF
GRANADA*, Part II.
THE REHEARSAL, by the Duke of
Buckingham and others.
Wycherley's *LOVE IN A WOOD.*

1672
Third Dutch War began (ended
1674).

Joseph Addison born.

Richard Steele born.

Dryden's *MARRIAGE À LA MODE.*

1674

New Drury Lane Theatre (King's Company) opened.

Death of Milton.

Nicholas Rowe born.

Thomas Rymer's *Reflections on Aristotle's Treatise of Poesy* (translation of Rapin) published.

1675

Dryden's *AURENG-ZEBE.*

Wycherley's *THE COUNTRY WIFE.**

1676

Etherege's *THE MAN OF MODE.*

Otway's *DON CARLOS.*

Shadwell's *THE VIRTUOSO.*

Wycherley's *THE PLAIN DEALER.*

1677

Behn's *THE ROVER.*

Dryden's *ALL FOR LOVE.*

Lee's *THE RIVAL QUEENS.*

Rymer's *Tragedies of the Last Age Considered* published.

1678

Popish Plot.

George Farquhar born.

Bunyan's *Pilgrim's Progress* (Part I) published.

1679

Exclusion Bill introduced.

Death of Thomas Hobbes.

Death of Roger Boyle, Earl of Orrery.

Charles Johnson born.

1680

Death of Samuel Butler.

Death of John Wilmot, Earl of Rochester.

Dryden's *THE SPANISH FRIAR.*
Lee's *LUCIUS JUNIUS BRUTUS.*
Otway's *THE ORPHAN.*

1681
Charles II dissolved Parliament at
Oxford.
Dryden's *Absalom and Achitophel*
published.
Tate's adaptation of *KING LEAR.*

1682
The King's and the Duke of York's
Companies merged into the United
Company.
Dryden's *The Medal, MacFlecknoe,*
and *Religio Laici* published.
Otway's *VENICE PRESERVED.*

1683
Rye House Plot.
Death of Thomas Killigrew.
Crowne's *THE CITY POLITI-
QUES.*

1685
Death of Charles II; accession of
James II.
Revocation of the Edict of Nantes.
The Duke of Monmouth's Re-
bellion.
Death of Otway.
John Gay born.
Crowne's *SIR COURTLY NICE.*
Dryden's *ALBION AND ALBAN-
IUS.*

1687
Death of the Duke of Buckingham.
Dryden's *The Hind and the Panther*
published.
Newton's *Principia* published.

1688
The Revolution.
Alexander Pope born.
Shadwell's *THE SQUIRE OF AL-
SATIA.*

1689

The War of the League of Augsburg
began (ended 1697).
Toleration Act.
Death of Aphra Behn.
Shadwell made Poet Laureate.
Dryden's *DON SEBASTIAN*.
Shadwell's *BURY FAIR*.

1690

Battle of the Boyne.
Locke's *Two Treatises of Government*
and *An Essay Concerning Human
Understanding* published.

Joins the United Company as
apprentice-actor.

1691

Death of Etherege.
Langbaine's *An Account of the English
Dramatic Poets* published.

1692

Death of Lee.
Death of Shadwell.
Tate made Poet Laureate.

1693

George Lillo born.*
Rymer's *A Short View of Tragedy*
published.
Congreve's *THE OLD BACHELOR*.

Marries Katherine Shore.

1694

Death of Queen Mary.
Southerne's *THE FATAL MAR-
RIAGE*.

1695

Group of actors led by Thomas
Betterton leave Drury Lane and
establish a new company at Lin-
coln's Inn Fields.
Congreve's *LOVE FOR LOVE*.
Southerne's *OROONOKO*.

1696

Vanbrugh's *THE RELAPSE*.   *LOVE'S LAST SHIFT*.

1697

Treaty of Ryswick ended the War
of the League of Augsburg.

Charles Macklin born.
Congreve's *THE MOURNING BRIDE.*
Vanbrugh's *THE PROVOKED WIFE.*

1698
Collier controversy started with the publication of *A Short View of the Immorality and Profaneness of the English Stage.*

1699
Farquhar's *THE CONSTANT COUPLE.*

1700
Death of Dryden.
Blackmore's *Satire Against Wit* published.
Congreve's *THE WAY OF THE WORLD.*

1701
Act of Settlement.
War of the Spanish Succession began (ended 1713).
Death of James II.
Rowe's *TAMERLANE.*
Steele's *THE FUNERAL.*

1702
Death of William III; accession of Anne.
The Daily Courant began publication.

SHE WOULD AND SHE WOULD NOT.

1703
Death of Samuel Pepys.
Rowe's *THE FAIR PENITENT.*

Son Theophilus born.

1704
Capture of Gibraltar; Battle of Blenheim.
Defoe's *The Review* began publication (1704–1713).
Swift's *A Tale of a Tub* and *The Battle of the Books* published.

THE CARELESS HUSBAND.

1705
Haymarket Theatre opened.
Steele's *THE TENDER HUSBAND.*

1706

Battle of Ramillies.

Farquhar's *THE RECRUITING OFFICER.*

1707

Union of Scotland and England.

Death of Farquhar.

Henry Fielding born.

Farquhar's *THE BEAUX' STRATAGEM.*

1708

Downes' *Roscius Anglicanus* published.

1709

Samuel Johnson born.

Rowe's edition of Shakespeare published.

The Tatler began publication (1709–1710).

Centlivre's *THE BUSY BODY.*

1710

Cibber, Wilks, and Dogget licensed as actor-managers of Drury Lane.

1711

Shaftesbury's *Characteristics* published.

The Spectator began publication (1711–1712).

Pope's *An Essay on Criticism* published.

1713

Treaty of Utrecht ended the War of the Spanish Succession.

Addison's *CATO.*

Daughter Charlotte born.

1714

Death of Anne; accession of George I.

Steele became Governor of Drury Lane.

John Rich assumed management of Lincoln's Inn Fields.

Centlivre's *THE WONDER: A WOMAN KEEPS A SECRET.*
Rowe's *JANE SHORE.*

1715
Jacobite Rebellion.
Death of Tate.
Rowe made Poet Laureate.
Death of Wycherley.

1716
Addison's *THE DRUMMER.*

1717
David Garrick born.   *THE NON-JUROR.*
Gay, Pope, and Arbuthnot's *THREE HOURS AFTER MARRIAGE.*

1718
Death of Rowe.
Centlivre's *A BOLD STROKE FOR A WIFE.*

1719
Death of Addison.
Defoe's *Robinson Crusoe* published.
Young's *BUSIRIS, KING OF EGYPT.*

1720
South Sea Bubble.
Samuel Foote born.
Steele suspended from the Governorship of Drury Lane (restored 1721).
Little Theatre in the Haymarket opened.
Steele's *The Theatre* (periodical) published.
Hughes' *THE SIEGE OF DAMASCUS.*

1721
Walpole became first Minister.

1722
Steele's *THE CONSCIOUS LOVERS.*

1723
Death of Susannah Centlivre.
Death of D'Urfey.

1725
Pope's edition of Shakespeare published.

1726
Death of Jeremy Collier.
Death of Vanbrugh.
Law's *Unlawfulness of Stage Entertainments* published.
Swift's *Gulliver's Travels* published.

1727
Death of George I; accession of George II.
Death of Sir Isaac Newton.
Arthur Murphy born.

1728
Pope's *The Dunciad* (First Version) published.
Gay's *THE BEGGAR'S OPERA*.

THE PROVOKED HUSBAND (expansion of Vanbrugh's fragment *A JOURNEY TO LONDON*).

1729
Goodman's Fields Theatre opened.
Death of Congreve.
Death of Steele.
Edmund Burke born.

1730
Oliver Goldsmith born.
Thomson's *The Seasons* published.
Fielding's *THE AUTHOR'S FARCE*.
Fielding's *TOM THUMB* (revised as *THE TRAGEDY OF TRAGEDIES*, 1731).

Made Poet Laureate.

1731
Death of Defoe.
Lillo's *THE LONDON MERCHANT*.
Fielding's *THE GRUB STREET OPERA*.

1732
Covent Garden Theatre opened.
Death of Gay.

Retires from active management of Drury Lane.

George Colman the elder born.
Fielding's *THE COVENT GAR-
DEN TRAGEDY.*
Fielding's *THE MODERN HUS-
BAND.*
Charles Johnson's *CAELIA.*

1733
Pope's *An Essay on Man* (Epistles
I–III) published (Epistle IV, 1734).

1734
Death of Dennis.
The Prompter began publication
(1734–1736).
Theobald's edition of Shakespeare
published.
Fielding's *DON QUIXOTE IN
ENGLAND.*

1736
Fielding led the "Great Mogul's
Company of Comedians" at the
Little Theatre in the Haymarket
(1736–1737).
Fielding's *PASQUIN.*
Lillo's *FATAL CURIOSITY.*

1737
The Stage Licensing Act.
Dodsley's *THE KING AND THE
MILLER OF MANSFIELD.*
Fielding's *THE HISTORICAL RE-
GISTER FOR 1736.*

1738
Johnson's *London* published.
Pope's *One Thousand Seven Hundred
and Thirty-Eight* published.
Thomson's *AGAMEMNON.*

1739
War with Spain began.
Death of Lillo.
Hugh Kelly born.
Fielding's *The Champion* began pub-
lication (1739–1741).

Johnson's *Complete Vindication of Licensers of the Stage*, an ironical criticism of the Licensing Act, published after Brooke's *GUSTAVUS VASA* was denied a license.

1740

War of the Austrian Succession began (ended 1748).
James Boswell born.
Richardson's *Pamela* published.
Garrick's *LETHE*.
Thomson and Mallet's *ALFRED*.

Apology for the Life of Colley Cibber published.

1741

Edmund Malone born.
Garrick began acting.
Fielding's *Shamela* published.
Garrick's *THE LYING VALET*.

1742

Walpole resigned his offices.
Fielding's *Joseph Andrews* published.
Pope's *New Dunciad* (Book IV of *The Dunciad*) published.
Young's *The Complaint, or Night Thoughts* published (additional parts published each year until 1745).

Letters to Mr. Pope published.

1743

Death of Henry Carey.
Fielding's *Miscellanies* published.
Pope's *The Dunciad* (final version) published.

Pope makes Cibber central figure in revised *Dunciad*.

1744

Death of Pope.
Death of Theobald.
Dodsley's *A Select Collection of Old Plays* published.
Johnson's *Life of Mr. Richard Savage* published.

1745

Jacobite Rebellion.
Death of Swift.
Thomas Holcroft born.
Johnson's *Observations on Macbeth* published.

Failure of his last play, *PAPAL TYRANNY*.

Thomson's *TANCRED AND SIGIS-MUNDA*.

1746

Death of Southerne.

Collins's *Odes* published.

1747

Garrick entered the management of Drury Lane Theatre.

Johnson's *Prologue Spoken by Mr. Garrick at the Opening of the Theatre in Drury Lane, 1747*.

Warburton's edition of Shakespeare published.

Garrick's *MISS IN HER TEENS*.

Hoadley's *THE SUSPICIOUS HUS-BAND*.

1748

Treaty of Aix-la-Chapelle ended the War of the Austrian Succession.

Death of Thomson.

Hume's *Philosophical Essays Concerning Human Understanding* published.

Richardson's *Clarissa* published.

Smollett's *Roderick Random* published.

1749

Death of Ambrose Philips.

Bolingbroke's *Idea of a Patriot King* published.

Chetwood's *A General History of the Stage* published.

Fielding's *Tom Jones* published.

Johnson's *The Vanity of Human Wishes* published.

Hill's *MEROPE* (adaptation of Voltaire).

Johnson's *IRENE*.

1750

Death of Aaron Hill.

Johnson's *The Rambler* began publication (1750–1752).

1751

Death of Bolingbroke.

Richard Brinsley Sheridan born.

Gray's *An Elegy Wrote in a Country Churchyard* published.

Smollett's *Peregrine Pickle* published.

1752

Fielding's *Amelia* published.

Fielding's *The Covent Garden Journal* published.

Mason's *ELFRIDA* published.

1753

Death of Bishop Berkeley.

Elizabeth Inchbald born.

Foote's *THE ENGLISHMAN IN PARIS*.

Glover's *BOADICEA*.

Moore's *THE GAMESTER*.

Young's *THE BROTHERS*.

1754

Death of Fielding.

Richardson's *Sir Charles Grandison* published.

Whitehead's *CREUSA, QUEEN OF ATHENS*.

1755

Fielding's *Voyage to Lisbon* published.

Johnson's *A Dictionary of the English Language* published.

John Brown's *BARBAROSSA*.

1756

Seven Years War began.

William Godwin born.

Burke's *A Philosophical Enquiry into . . . the Sublime and Beautiful* published.

First part of Joseph Warton's *Essay on . . . Pope* published (second part, 1782).

Murphy's *THE APPRENTICE*.

1757

Battle of Plassey (India).   Death.

Death of Moore.
William Blake born.
Gray's *Odes* published.
Home's *DOUGLAS* (performed the
year before in Edinburgh).